P9-CKY-767

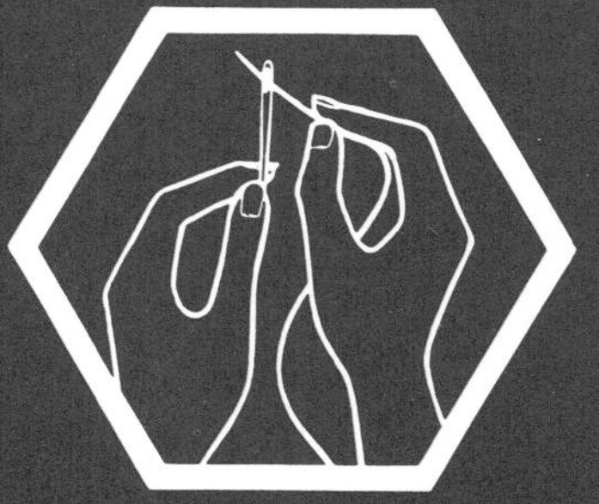

A *Golden Hands* PATTERN BOOK

EMBROIDERY

A Golden Hands PATTERN BOOK

EMBROIDERY

RANDOM HOUSE NEW YORK

 Published in the United States by Random House, Inc., New York, and simultaneously in Canada by Random House of Canada Limited, Toronto.
The greater part of the material published in this book was first published by Marshall Cavendish Ltd. in "Golden Hands." The British edition entitled *The Golden Hands Book of Embroidery* was published by William Collins Sons & Co Ltd.

Library of Congress Cataloging in Publication Data
Embroidery: a Golden hands pattern book.
Originally published under title: The Golden hands book of embroidery.
"The greater part of the material published in this book was first published ... in 'Golden hands.' "
1. Embroidery—Patterns. I. Golden hands.
TT771.G6 1973 746.4'4 72-11423
ISBN 0-394-48577-7

Manufactured in the United States of America
9 8 7 6 5 4 3 2

CONTENTS

About this book . . .

Whether you are an expert or a beginner in the art of embroidery, to leaf through this book will be a mouth-watering experience.

There is something for everyone in this collection which includes modern, original designs for fashion accessories, bedspreads, tablecloths, pillows, children's toys, framed pictures, rugs and place mats. Each design is accompanied by straightforward easy-to-follow instructions and, if you have never put needle to fabric before, there is a stitch guide on pages 126–128 explaining how all the stitches in the book are worked. There is also a technical know-how section on pages 121–125 that explains, among other things, how to finish and make up your work.

We have suggested a wide variety of new and beautiful fabrics and threads for you to work with, as well as the more traditional embroidery materials. Many of the designs can be completed with encouraging speed. So, if this is your first attempt at embroidery—or if leisure time is short—choose one of the designs involving only one or two colors and a simple technique to start with. You can work your way up to the more advanced and intricate patterns we have chosen for the experienced embroiderer.

We have also included a special section on pages 98 – 103 on how to go about creating your own designs. This should open up a completely new area of creative activity and satisfaction.

Patterns. There are three types of patterns for you to use: trace patterns, graphs and charts. Explanatory notes and diagrams showing how to employ these methods, together with instructions for making each of the projects, may be found on pages 121-125.

Materials. Material requirements are arranged in the following way. For example: D.M.C. six-strand floss. **1.** 666 scarlet (4). D.M.C. is the name of the thread. Six-strand floss is the type. The first number (in this case, **1**) refers to the area on the pattern where the thread is to be used, followed by the manufacturer's color number (666) and the color description (scarlet). The last figure in parentheses refers to the approximate number of skeins, cards or balls of thread you will need. Therefore, you should purchase 4 skeins of D.M.C.'s scarlet six-strand floss, color number 666 for area **1** of the chart, tracing pattern or graph.

Colors. Precise color references are recommended for certain designs—as, for instance, with the shading of leaves and flowers, where the relationship between tones is important. However, with most other designs, color is entirely a matter of personal preference, Remember to be generous in your choice of threads. Embroidery should always be rich and vivid.

Stitches. The fully illustrated Stitch Library on pages 126-128 may be used by both new and experienced embroiderers for instruction or as a ready-reference guide. In many of the designs, we suggest that stitches be worked in a free and impressionistic manner, rather than being restricted to a set form. And you'll soon notice that embroidery stitches can be made to work for you creatively—just as paint can work creatively for the artist. For example, flat stitches catch the light, so by changing the type of stitch and the direction in which you work it, you can alter color tone easily—and give your work extra perspective. Let your imagination go. You'll enjoy watching your embroidery come alive.

If you have any difficulty in obtaining the yarns quoted locally, write to the manufacturers below for details of your nearest retailer.

D.M.C. threads via Merribee Needlecraft Co., 4904 West Lancaster, Fort Worth, Texas 76107

Columbia-Minerva yarns via V.I.P. Yarns, c/o The Mill Outlet Store, East Penn Avenue, Robesonia, Pennsylvania 19551

Bucilla yarns via Bernhard Ulmann Co., 30-20 Thomson Avenue, Long Island City, New York 11101

Appleton yarns via American Crewel Studios, P.O. Box 1756, Point Pleasant Beach, New Jersey 08742

Credits: Photographs by Camera Press GMN, pages 10, 11, 12, 13, 15, 25, 28, 76, 77, 86. Kjell Nilsson, pages 9, 22, 24, 25, 26, 27, 29, 32, 33, 94, 95.
H. Von Sterneck, page 15.
Seiden & Almgren, page 18.
Ed-foto, pages 16, 17, 20, 21, 97. IMS. page 23. Svante Sjostedt, page 97.
Art work by Paul Williams.
Pear designs by Pat Phillpott.
Cover photograph by Chris Lewis.

DESIGN COLLECTION

80 beautiful patterns to embroider

1

A gay lady bug purse to work in rich colors. *See chart on page 39.*

2

Work this garland of tiny sprays of ribbon- tied roses to make an attractive centerpiece. Tracing pattern on page 40.

3

Spring blossoms scattered over delicate organdy make elegant table mats. Tracing pattern on page 41.

4

Summer sprigs of flowers adorn a circular organdy tablecloth, bias-trimmed to pick out one of the embroidery colors. Tracing pattern on pages 40-41.

Full of texture and pretty as a picture—a colorful posy bowl. Tracing patterns on pages 42-43.

A classical Hungarian design of pigeons in a plum tree. Tracing pattern on pages 44-45.

Clever use of color and shading make this framed rose panel look like a Redouté print. Place the two buds at points A and B on the tracing pattern on page 46.

As single initials or combined into a monogram, this attractive alphabet can be used to individualize fashion accessories or table linen. Tracing pattern on page 47.

A bold design for a big bedspread. The medallion pattern, worked in chain stitch, gives maximum effect for minimum work. Graph pattern on pages 48-49.

10–16

You can use these seven designs of fruits, berries and flowers either combined for a framed picture, or separately on table napkins or place mats.

Trace patterns on pages 50-51.

Finished measurement: About 18″ x 12″ Each motif is about 5″ x 5″.
Fabric: Cream linen 19½″ x 13½″.
Threads: D.M.C. 6-strand floss, one skein of each color. **1.** 648 silver gray; **2.** 436 light brown; **3.** 610 dark brown; **4.** 730 olive green; **5.** 471 mid green; **6.** white; **7.** 743 yellow; **8.** 970 orange; **9.** 948 beige pink; **10.** 469 dark green; **11.** 645 dark gray; **12.** 646 mid gray; **13.** 472 light green; **14.** 602 cyclamen; **15.** 309 red; **16.** 917 plum; **17.** 553 mauve. Use two strands in the needle.
Needles: Crewel, No. 7.
Stitches: Chain, French knots, stem.

The fabric amount given is sufficient to work the fruits as a framed panel. Use single motifs on place mats or work them side by side as a repeating border on a tablecloth. Trace the designs onto the fabric as explained on page 121. Work the circular stitching on the fruits from the outside to the center. Add the French knots to the strawberry when the stem stitch filling is complete. Make up for framing as shown on page 122.

17

A rampant lion—appliquéd on washable terry cloth—makes an exciting child's bedspread.
Graph pattern on page 52.

18

These bright wild flowers worked in a free and easy way with simple stitches are typical of the relaxed modern style of Scandinavian embroidery.
Tracing pattern on page 53.

19-30

Add a personal touch to the presents you give with these Signs of the Zodiac. Tracing patterns on pages 54-55.

Finished measurement: About $4\frac{1}{2}'' \times 4\frac{1}{2}''$.
Fabric: Off-white linen 6″ x 6″.
Threads: D.M.C. 6-strand floss, one skein of each color. Use three strands in the needle.
Needles: Crewel, No. 6.
Stitches: Chain, detached chain, stem, buttonhole wheel, cross-stitch, French knots.

Embroider your birth sign with the part skeins of thread left from other projects. Use a range of tones similar to those illustrated for the best effect. Black or dark brown enhances the rich colors.
Transfer the motif to the fabric as shown on page 121. Each design is filled with rows of stem or chain stitch. The French knots are worked over the previously worked stitches. The scales of the fish are worked in cross-stitch, the crosses tied down with a short stitch. Buttonhole wheels form the skirt of Aquarius. For an unusual birthday card, mount as shown on page 122 and back with a double fold of stiff paper.

31

Appliqué apples—an easy way to add a splash of color to plain fabric. Cut out the apple and leaf shapes from the tracing patterns below. Then apply the shapes with either buttonhole stitch or pin stitch to the background fabric. Work the stem in satin stitch; the calyx, with three detached chain stitches.

32

Two Hungarian panels which you can either work separately on pockets, combine into a group of four on a pillow, or enlarge for a tote bag. *Tracing patterns on page 57.*

33

34

The Pimpernel Rose design, worked here in various sizes and shades of red, adapts well to the form of a round pillow. *See pattern and chart on pages 58-59.*

Finished measurement: About 10″ diameter.
Fabric: White linen approximately 12″ square. Bright pink linen 11″ square. Strip of pink linen for gusset $2\frac{1}{2}'' \times 34''$ long.
Threads: D.M.C. 6-strand floss; 1) 5 skeins 320—rose madder; 2) 3 skeins 606—flame; 3) 2 skeins 351—geranium; 4) 2 skeins 734—muscat green.
Needles: Crewel No. 7.
Stitches: French knot, long and short, and stem.

Prepare the fabric and transfer the design as on page 121. Work with 2 strands of thread and fill the flowers with long and short stitch as shown. Cover ground closely for the flat, rich effect of the flowers and outline in stem stitch. Work stem stitch on the tracing line of the two flowers with unfilled petals. Long and short stitch fills the centers. Press and finish as given on page 124.

35, 36

A floral alphabet and Wild Rose to work in various ways and sizes. *Alphabet pattern on pages 60-61.*

Finished measurement: Alphabet sampler, about 15″ x 16″.
Fabric: Yellow/green linen, 17″ x 18″.
Threads: D.M.C. 6-strand floss. 10 skeins 336 indigo; 10 skeins 798 cornflower; 1 skein 307 buttercup; 4 skeins 367 laurel green.
Needles: Crewel, No. 7.
Stitches: Long and short, satin, stem.

The alphabet sampler in two tones of blue on yellow/green linen is an attractive wall decoration. Transfer the design and mount the fabric in a frame as described on page 121. Work satin stitch for the letters and flower centers, long and short stitch for the flowers. Pad the satin stitch for a rich, raised effect. Use two strands of thread in the needle.

The letters have been used in individual colors and sizes to decorate the family dressing gowns.

To work the unusual bedspread, machine apply a large letter to the center. Combine it with flower embroidery in long and short and stem stitch. The colors match the round pillow. Use a hoop for the long and short stitch embroidery.

Instructions for the soft cushion with the yellow rose motif, shown in the lower picture on the left, are on page 59.

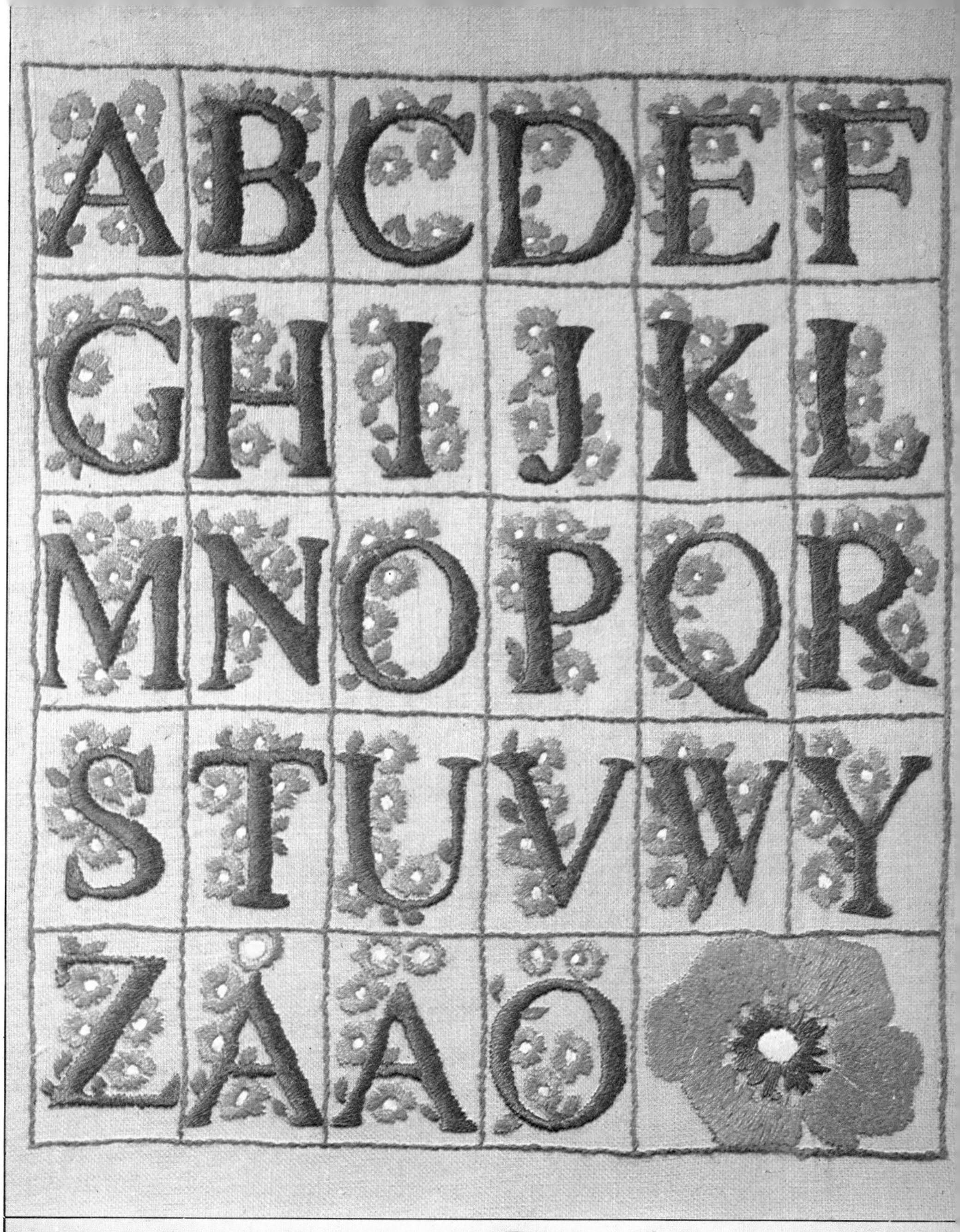

37 - 48

Pick your favorite wild plant from this collection of twelve species, and use it to decorate such things as pockets, purses and handbags. For napkins, tablemats or tray cloths, try choosing flowers to match the designs on your china. *Tracing patterns on pages 62-63.*

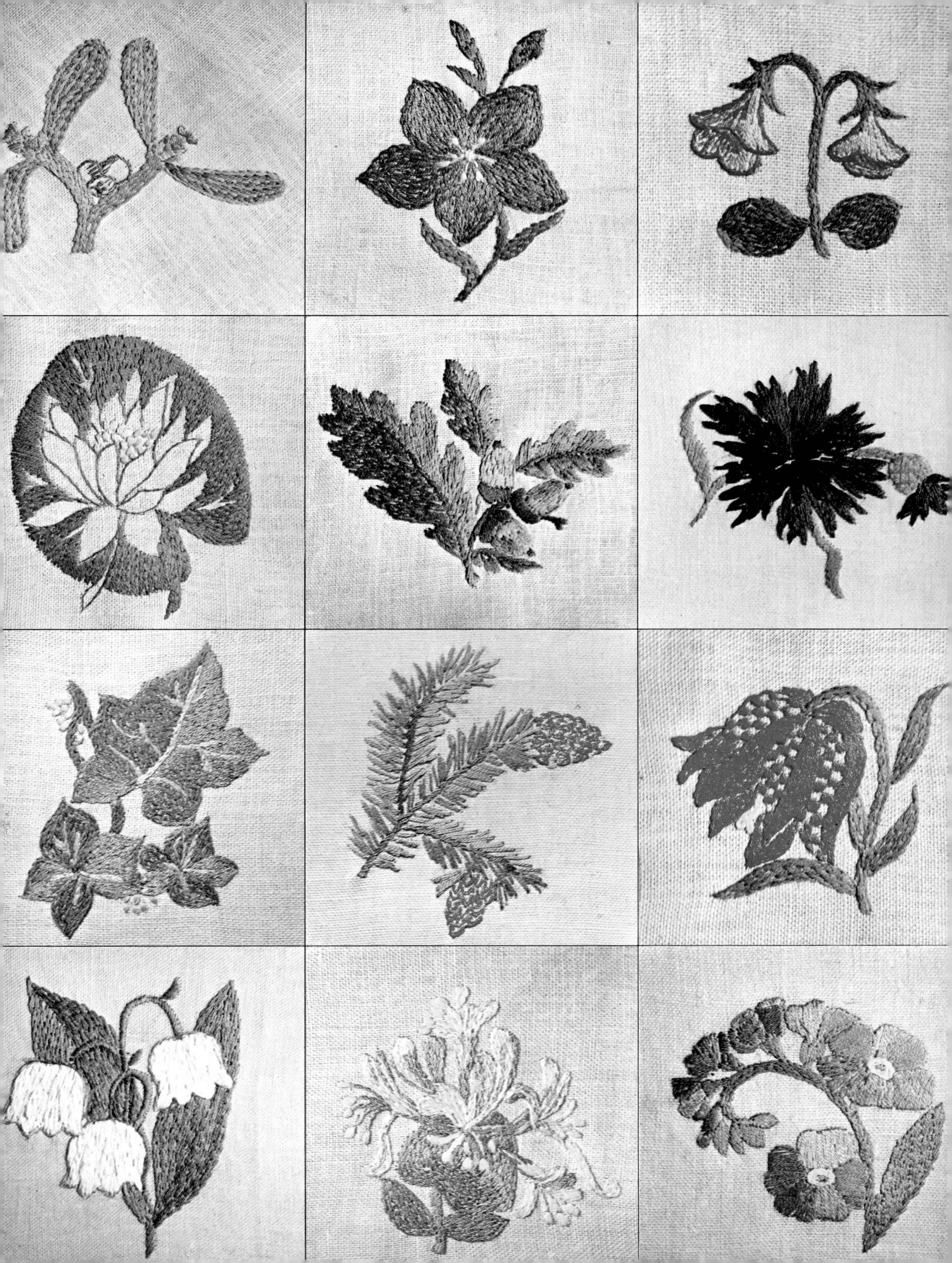

49

Clusters of bright white anemones cross-stitched on canvas give this stool a light, fresh touch. You can adapt the same design or repeat it for a matching pillow.
See chart on pages 64-65.

50

This Daisy rug is worked in one piece so that blocking and finishing it are simpler.
See chart on page 66.

This stylized picture "Blue Town" is worked in a range of blue-green shades with highlights of pink and white to create a cool and peaceful scene.
Graph patterns on page 67.

Finished Measurement: 18″ × $11\frac{1}{2}$″
Fabric: Dark green linen 23″ × 16″
Hardboard: 18″ × $11\frac{1}{2}$″
Needles: Crewel needle No. 8
Threads: D.M.C. 6-strand floss in following colors and amounts:
1. 7301 pale blue; **2.** 7800 light blue; **3.** 7306 medium blue; **4.** 7307 dark medium blue **5.** 7302 blue; **6.** 7318 light navy; **7.** 7996 turquoise; **8.** 7361 pale yellow; **9.** 7773 lime; **10.** 7431 light yellow; **11.** 7487 gold; **12.** 7387 dark green; **13.** 7389 very dark green; **14.** 7309 dark blue green; **15.** 7386 medium gray green; **16.** 7384 pale gray green; **17.** 7351 yellow green; **18.** 7226 mauve; **19.** 7228; deep mauve; **20.** 7241 dark slate blue; **21.** 7132 pale pink; **22.** 7133 deep pink; **23.** white; **24.** 7533 brown;

One skein each of colors:
6, 8, 9, 11, 12, 13, 16, 17, 18, 20, 21, 22, 23, 24
Two skeins each of colors:
1, 2, 3, 4, 5, 7, 10, 14, 15, 19

Stitches: running stitch. French knots and couching in a variety of simple methods. The flowers and leaves are in freely worked satin stitch. Use four strands in the needle for the French knots and layed threads, and two strands for the couching, and all other stitches. If preferred, small beads could be substituted for the French knots.

Trace pattern from chart on page 67 using the enlarging technique outlined on page 121.
It is essential to work this picture in a square embroidery frame to keep the stitching flat and even. When the work is completed, lay over a thick, soft pad and press carefully. Mount the picture as shown on page 122.

52

Brighten up a set of place mats with gay Mexican daisies, then give a personal touch by adding initials (see page 47) to the centers. Tracing pattern on page 68.

53

The basic Mexican daisy design, adapted as a picture. Cover the panel with heat-proof glass, and you have an attractive little tray. Tracing pattern on page 68.

54

A fashionably-laced belt, embroidered with the colorful daisy design. Tracing pattern on page 69.

55

Mexican daisies again—this time designed to fit neatly onto a glasses case. Tracing pattern on page 69.

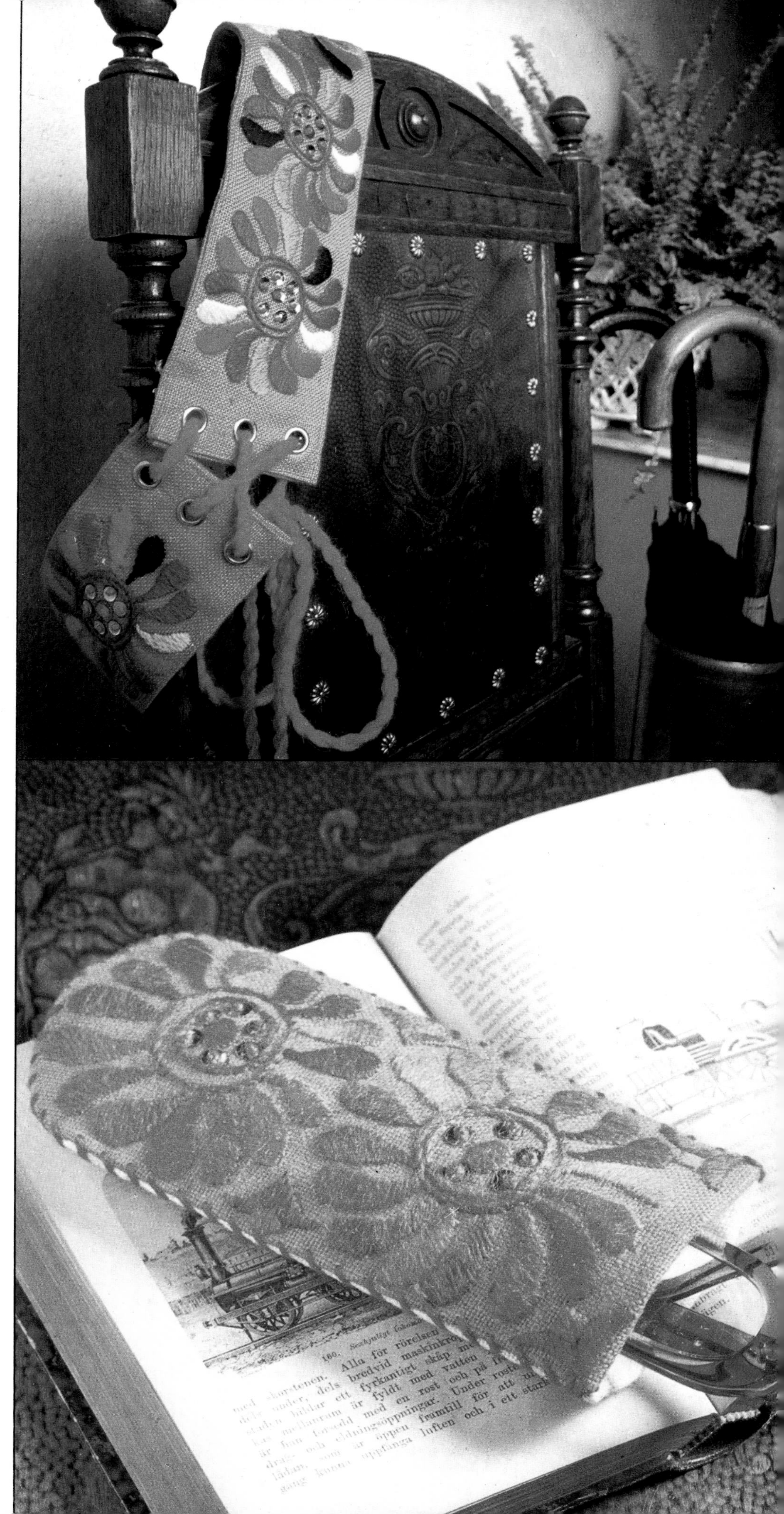

56

This charming design scatters small flowers over a stool and pillow cover with equal effect. *Tracing pattern on pages 70-71.*

A butterfly, embroidered and bejewelled in a range of muted tones, provides maximum impact as a framed wall panel. *Tracing pattern on page 72.*

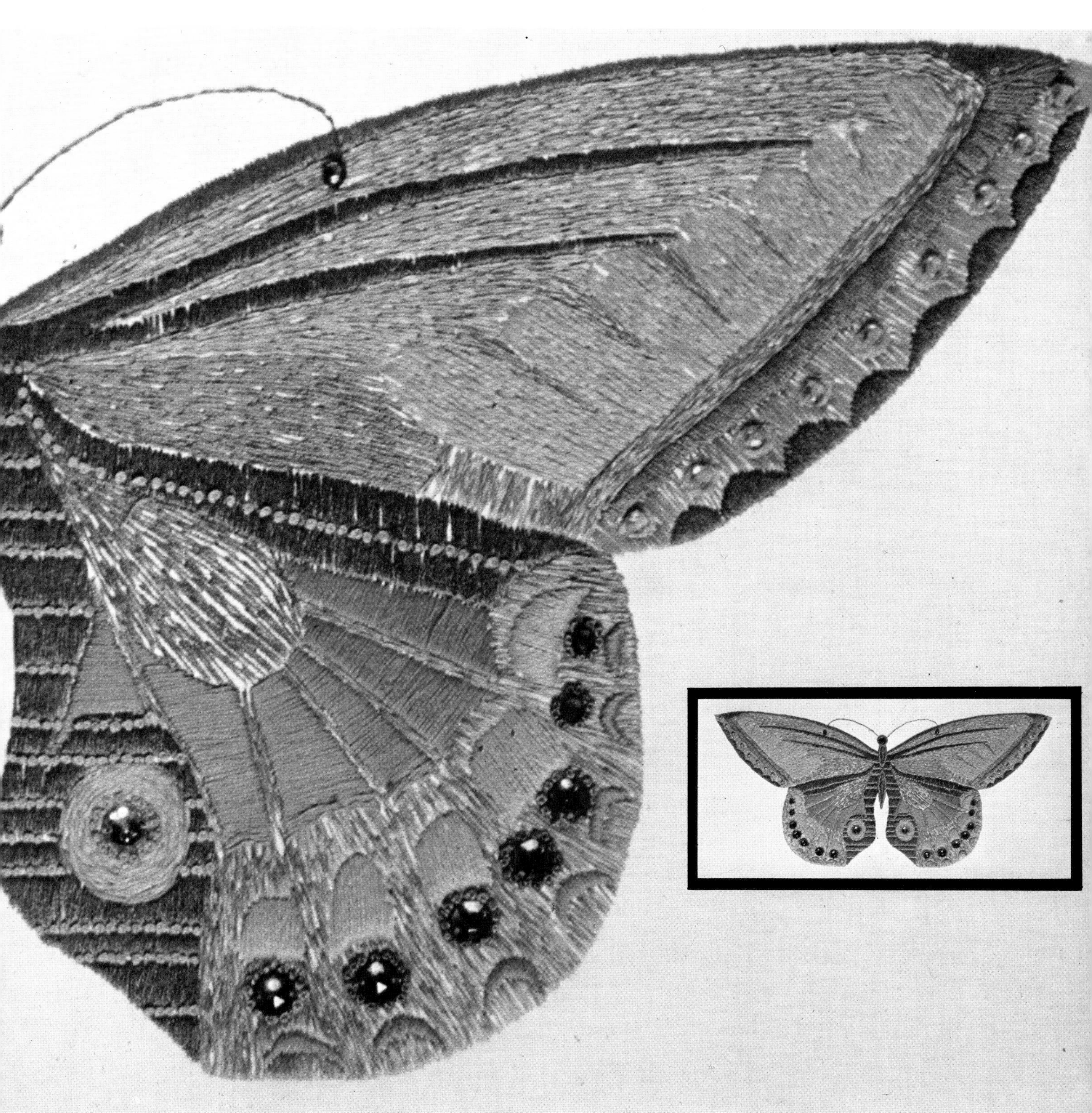

58

Motifs such as this simple pansy can be used and adapted for a wide variety of canvas work.

Finished measurement: 22″ × 11″
Fabric: 16″ × 15″ single weave with 10 threads to 1 inch
Threads: Matte embroidery cotton in orange, red, white and green
D.M.C. Pearl Pattern No. 1 in scarlet

Stitch: Cross-stitch
Mark the center of the rectangle of canvas each way with lines of basting stitches. Work in cross-stitch over two threads of canvas each way, following the designs from the center of the chart.

Worked on large mesh canvas over more threads, the motif is suitable for rugs, cushions or panels. Reduced, it could be used for curtain tie-back motifs and stool tops. As a petit point design, it looks pretty in miniature.

Instructions to complete the previous pages

I

Lady bug purse

Finished measurement: About $4\frac{1}{2}''$ x $6''$.
Fabric: Canvas – 16 threads to the inch. 14″ x 11″. Purse frame. Lining 14″ x 11″.
Threads: Bucilla Crewel Wool .Two cards of each color, 3 cards for the background.
1. 33 royal blue; **2.** 36 dark red; **3.** 86 fuchsia; **4.** 1 white (background).
Needles: Tapestry No. 20.
Stitches: Cross-stitch.

The embroidery is worked in cross-stich over two threads of canvas. Use three strands in the needle. Mark the centers of the canvas in each direction. Begin at the center and work outward to work the first row of the pattern. Stitch to fit the shape of the purse frame. Complete the pattern by working one row below another. Work in one piece, reversing the design for the second side. Block and make up with an interlining as shown on page 122. Overcast with strong thread through the punched holes in the metal frame.

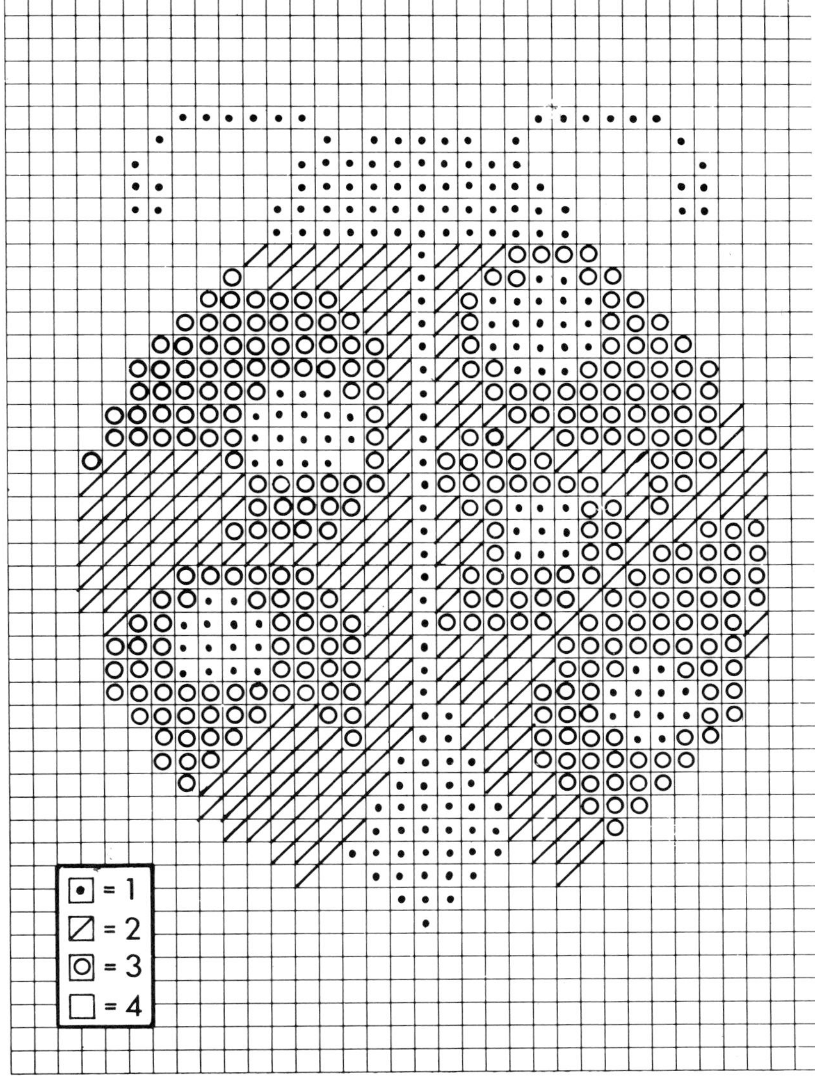

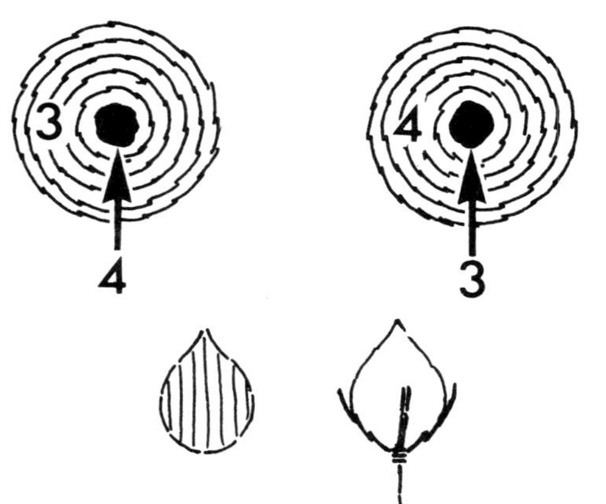

2 *Garland with ribbons*

Finished measurement: 11½″ diameter.
Fabric: Yellow/green linen, 13½″ square.
Threads: D.M.C. 6-strand floss, one skein of each. **1.** 519 peacock blue; **2.** 733 muscat green; **3.** 666 scarlet; **4.** 899 rose pink; **5.** 912 laurel green.
Needles: Crewel, No. 6.
Stitches: Buttonhole, French knot, satin and stem.

A tiny flower spray is worked as a repeating motif to encircle the mat. Around the outer edge is a row of stem stitch.
Work with three strands of floss.
Follow the instructions on page 121 for tracing the design onto the fabric. Trace the hem line and a cutting line ½″ outside it. The stem stitch flowers are worked from the outside of the circle in a spiral toward the center. This will be more easily worked in a hoop. Work the stitches closely but not too small. Work the leaves in buttonhole stitch and the buds in satin stitch. Work three straight stitches in green, over the satin stitch buds. Embroider a row of stem stitch on the hemline. Press and make up as shown on page 123.

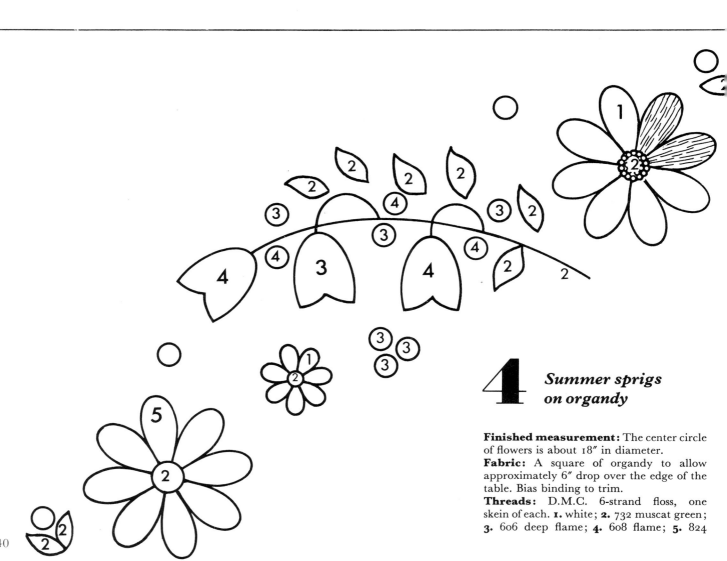

4 *Summer sprigs on organdy*

Finished measurement: The center circle of flowers is about 18″ in diameter.
Fabric: A square of organdy to allow approximately 6″ drop over the edge of the table. Bias binding to trim.
Threads: D.M.C. 6-strand floss, one skein of each. **1.** white; **2.** 732 muscat green; **3.** 606 deep flame; **4.** 608 flame; **5.** 824

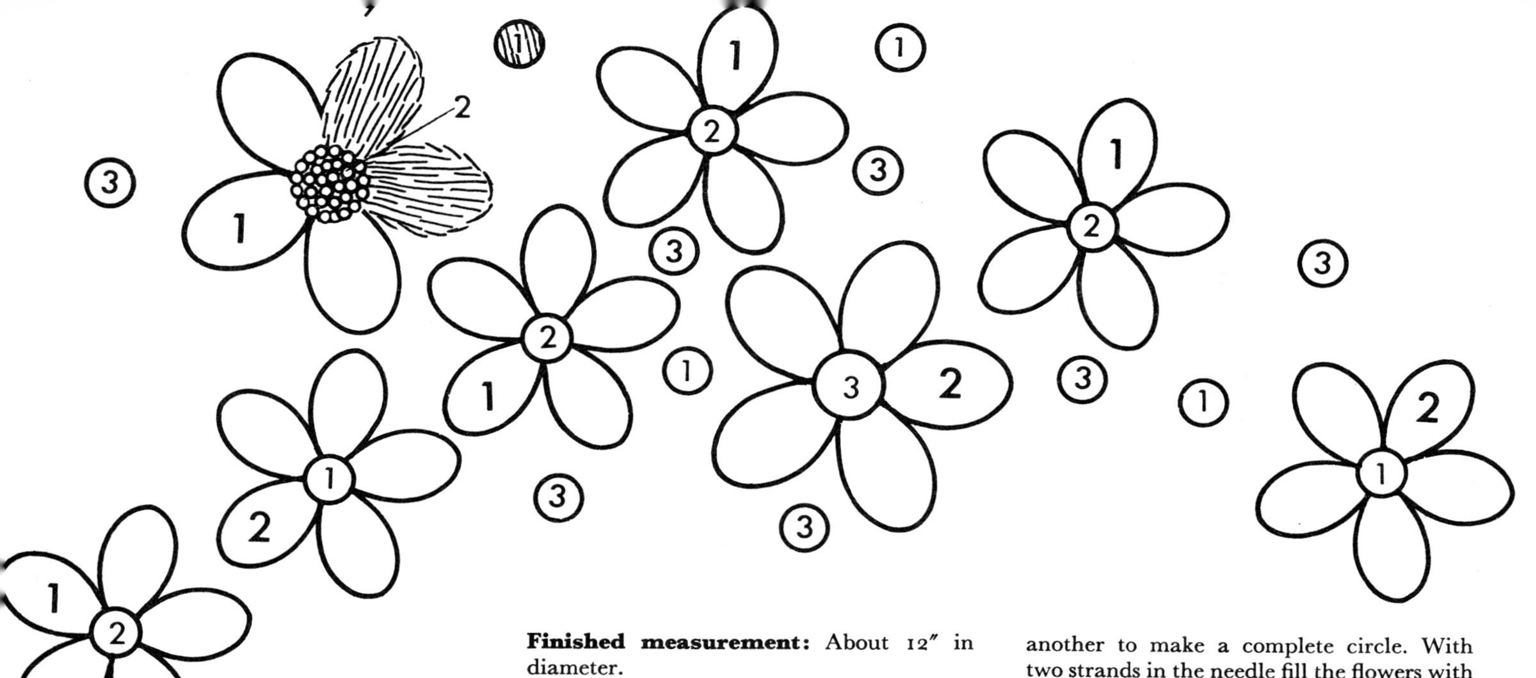

Finished measurement: About 12″ in diameter.
Fabric: White organdy, 14″ square.
Threads: D.M.C. 6-strand floss. **1.** 3 skeins 742 buttercup; **2.** 3 skeins white; **3.** 1 skein 3347 light moss green.
Needles: Crewel, No. 7.
Stitches: French knot, long and short, stem and satin.

3 *First flowers of spring*

Trace the design onto the fabric as described on page 121, with one section following another to make a complete circle. With two strands in the needle fill the flowers with long and short shading. Finish each flower with a stem stitch outline and fill the center with French knots. Work the satin stitch spots. Fasten off the thread for each one. Threads carried across from one place to another will show through the transparent fabric and spoil the delicacy of the design. Work a row of stem stitch at the hemline. Press and make up following instructions on pages 122, 123.

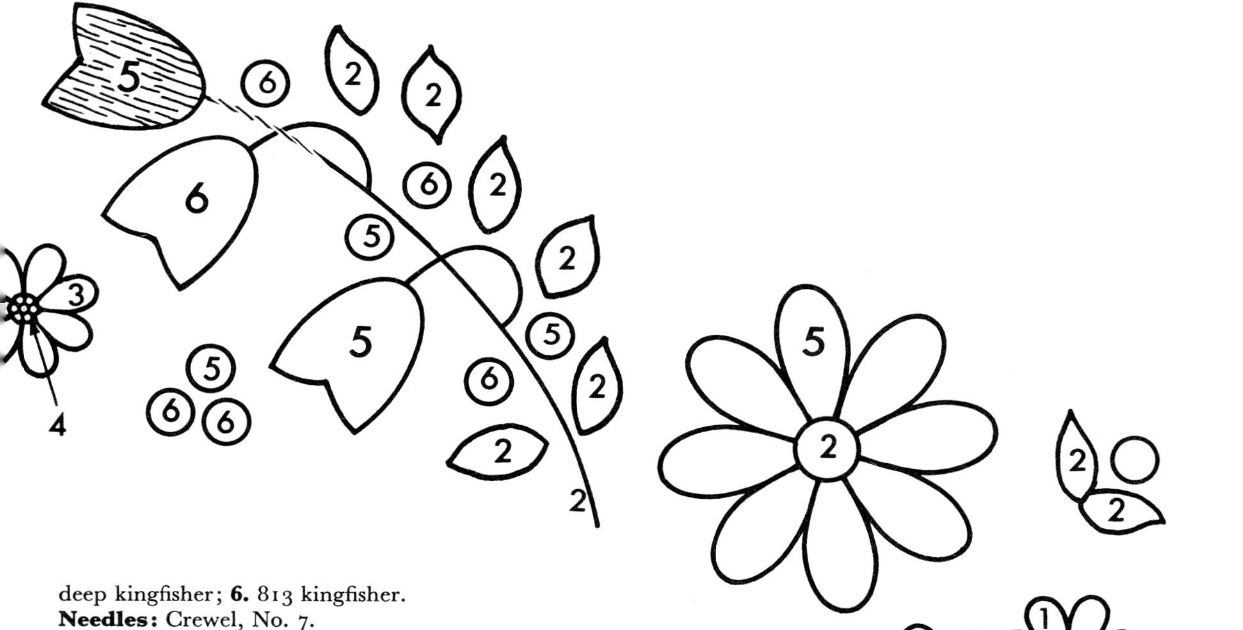

deep kingfisher; **6.** 813 kingfisher.
Needles: Crewel, No. 7.
Stitches: French knots, long and short, satin and stem.

Prepare the fabric as described on page 121. Work with two strands of floss throughout. Embroider the single flowers from the outer edges of the petals to the center. The bluebells are worked from the top to the base. Begin at the highest point of the petal in each case. Finish off each flower and leaf. A thread passing across the back of the fabric obscures the clarity of the design. Trim with colored bias binding. Press and finish as shown on pages 122, 123.

5 *Posy bowl*

Finished measurement: About 11″ x 14″.
Fabric: Lime green linen 13″ x 16″.
Threads: D.M.C. 6-strand floss, one skein of each color. **1.** white; **2.** 415 gray; **3.** 742 buttercup; **4.** 608 flame; **5.** 606 deep flame; **6.** 321 turkey red; **7.** 554 light cyclamen; **8.** 553 cyclamen; **9.** 601 magenta; **10.** 600 deep magenta; **11.** 816 raspberry. Use two strands in the needle for No. 1 and 7-11. Three strands for 2-7.
Needles: Crewel, No. 7 for two strands of thread. Crewel No. 6 for three strands.
Stitches: Chain, French knots, long and short, satin.

The bowl of flowers is embroidered in a subtle range of colors. A professional finishing touch is given by the red painted frame. It picks up the color of one of the flowers.

Trace the design onto the fabric as shown on page 121. The bowl is slightly left of center. Use an embroidery frame for the best results. Begin by working any parts of the design which lie underneath: e.g. the bowl and some of the flowers. Allow the stitching which overlays it to encroach slightly. Prepare for framing as shown on page 122.

Pigeons in a plum tree

Finished measurement: About 10″ x 12″.
Fabric: White linen, medium weight. 12$\frac{1}{2}$″ x 14$\frac{1}{2}$″
Threads: D.M.C. Tapestry yarn, 3 skeins each of: **1.** 7346 dark green; **2.** 7342 green; 2 skeins of: **3.** 7797 blue; and 1 skein each of: **4.** 7107 red; **5.** 7602 rose; **6.** 7947 orange; **7.** 7508 brown. Black for eyes and beaks of birds.
Needle: Chenille, No. 20.
Stitches: Chain, Satin, Stem.

Birds perched among the branches of trees and flowers are a part of the traditional design of Hungary. The birds in this framed picture are embroidered in chain and stem stitch and perch among satin stitch leaves. Transfer the design and mount the fabric in a frame as described on page 121. The leaves and berries are worked in satin stitch. Follow the diagram for the direction of stitch. For a contrasting texture, work the leaves in surface satin stitch and the berries in padded satin stitch.
Press and prepare for framing as shown on page 122.

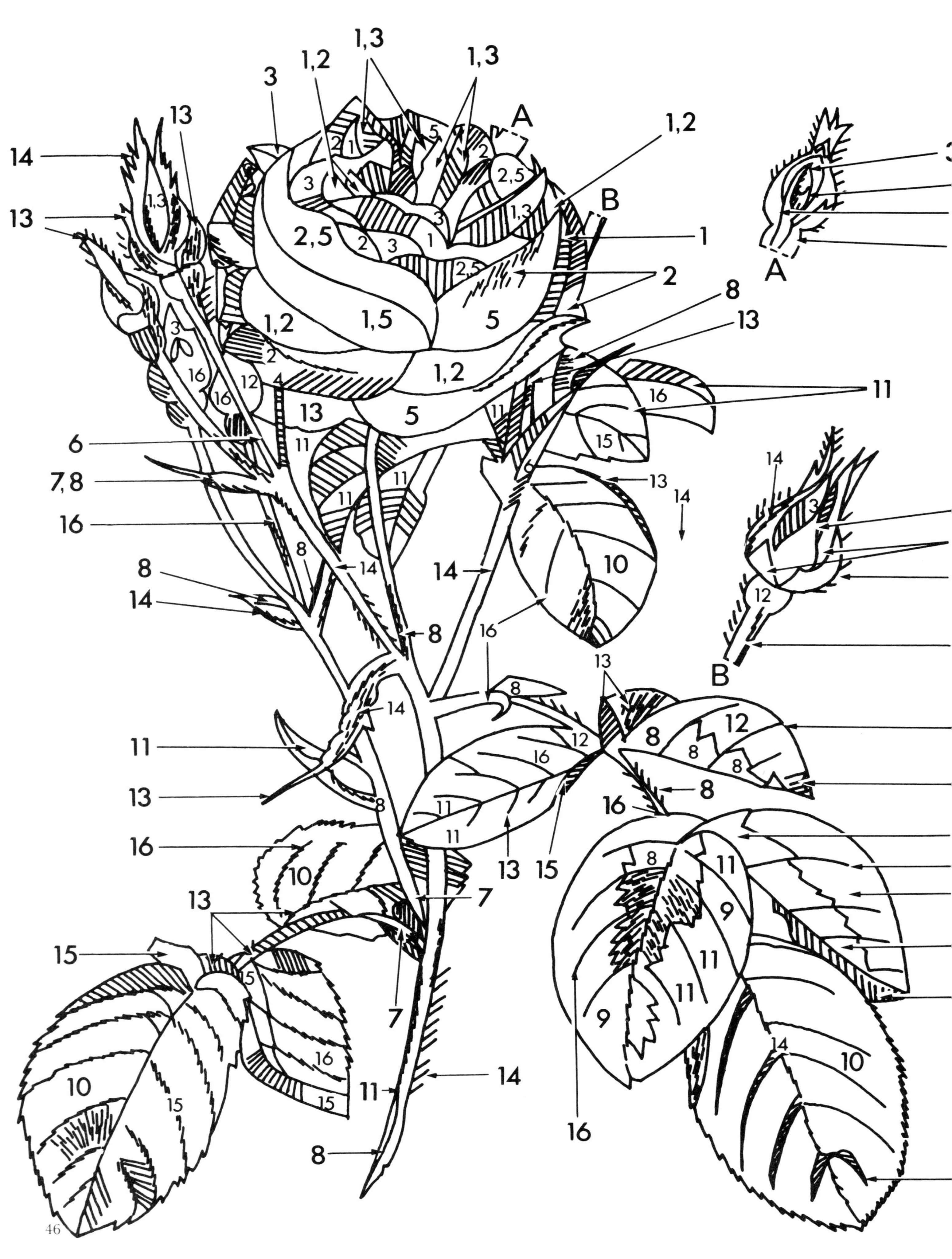
1,3
1,3
3
1,2
13
A
1,2
14
3
2
1
5
2
2,5
13
1,3
B
3
1
3
1,3
2,5
2
3
1
2,5
2
1,2
1,5
5
8
13
2
1,2
16
11
12
4
16
13
5
11
15
6
11
13
14
7,8
11
11
16
8
14
10
8
14
14
8
16
13
14
B
8
11
12
8
12
16
8
8
13
8
16
16
10
11
11
13
15
7
8
11
9
13
15
7
11
15
11
9
14
10
10
16
14
15
16
15
11
8
16
46

7 *Redouté-style rose spray*

Finished measurement: About 13" x 9".
Fabric: White linen, 15½" x 11½".
Threads: D.M.C. 6-strand floss, one skein of each color. **1.** 818 pink; **2.** 819 light rose; **3.** 891 rose madder; **4.** 335 deep pink; **5.** 818 light pink; **6.** 400 oak brown; **7.** 725 mid-brown; **8.** 783 brown; **9.** 905 deep green; **10.** 906 parrot green; **11.** 702 grass green; **12.** 3345 moss green; **13.** 937 almond green; **14.** 470 mid-green; **15.** 369 light green; **16.** 3348 light moss green.
Needles: Crewel, Nos. 7 and 8.
Stitches: Feather, long and short, satin and stem.

Trace the design onto the fabric as described on page 121. The leaves can be traced as a smooth line. The serrated edge is suggested in the embroidery. For ease of working, mount the fabric in a frame. With one strand in the needle, shade the leaves as suggested in the diagram. Work stem stitch veins over the finished leaf. The flower is worked with two strands. Begin at the center and work one petal over another. Work from the high point of each, shaping it toward the growing point. Finish the stem stitch stems with half feather stitch thorns. Press and make up as shown on page 122.

Embroider a monogram 8

Thread: 1 skein D.M.C. 6-strand floss.
Needle: Crewel, No. 7.

Add a distinctive monogram to your favorite accessories. Trace the required letter according to the directions on page 121. The placing is important. Some suggestions are illustrated. Two strands of floss in the needle will be needed for a medium weight fabric. Work the embroidery in stem stitch over the single line. Slant the needle to a more acute angle as you work so that the stitch widens to satin stitch for the double lines.

2
1
2
CENTER

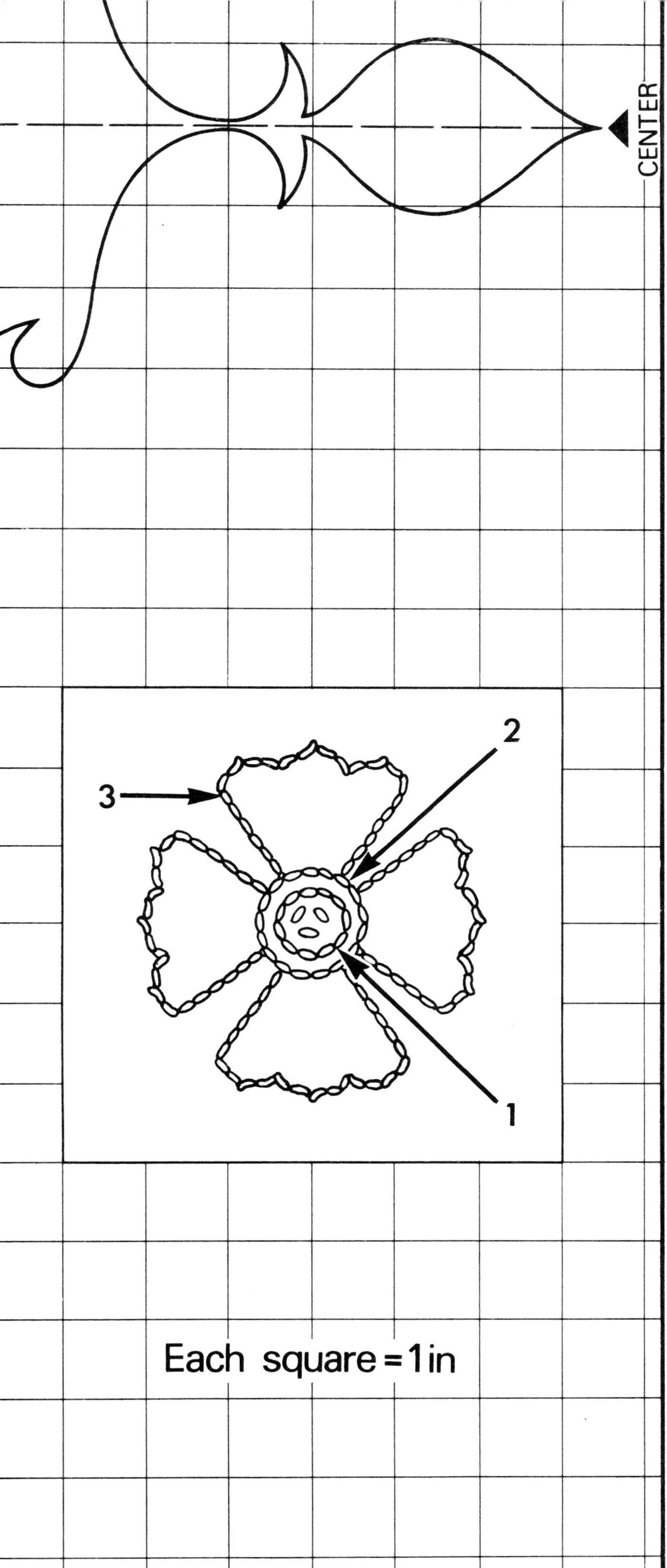

9 *Chain stitch bedspread*

Finished measurement: About 70" x 100" (to fit single bed).
Fabric: Cotton twill sheeting by the yard. 7½ yards of white cotton fringe to finish.
Threads: D.M.C. Matte Embroidery cotton. **1.** 9 skeins 2740 tangerine; **2.** 6 skeins 2444 yellow; **3.** 4 skeins 2797 blue.
Needle: Chenille, No. 18.
Stitch: Chain.

A design of classic simplicity. It is embroidered in chain stitch to enhance the effect of the flowing curves. The same design is worked successfully on a tablecloth. From the instructions on page 121 enlarge the design and place it in the center of the fabric. Take particular care in outlining the curves. The well-drawn line is the secret of the crisp finish. Work in chain stitch. On the tight curves, work the stitches smaller. At the points of the design, finish the line with a tying-down stitch as in detached chain and begin again into the stitch below. (See stitch library, page 127). Make up as shown on page 123. Work the orange border 2 inches in from the hem along the sides and foot.

10-16

Fruits, berries and flowers

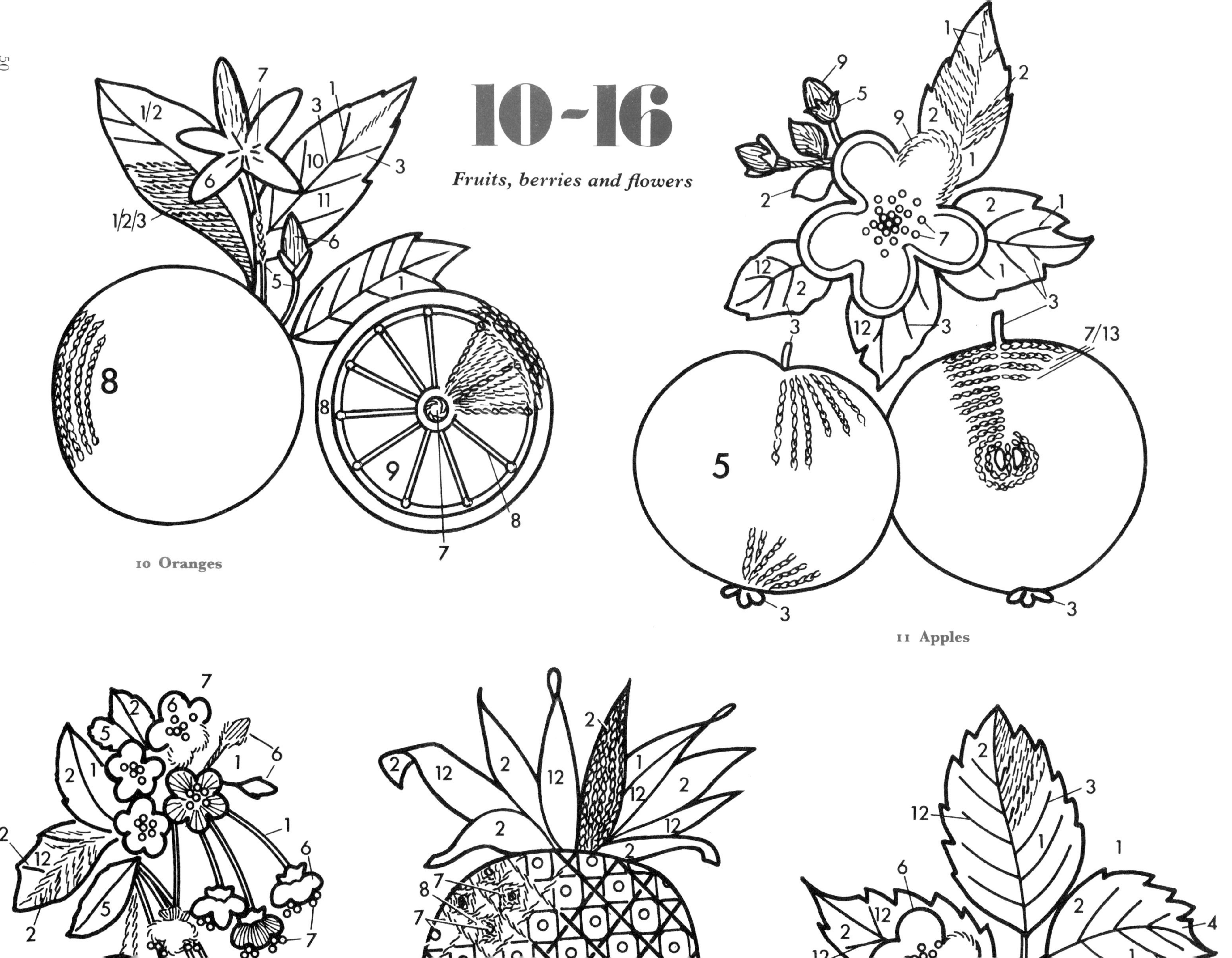

10 Oranges

11 Apples

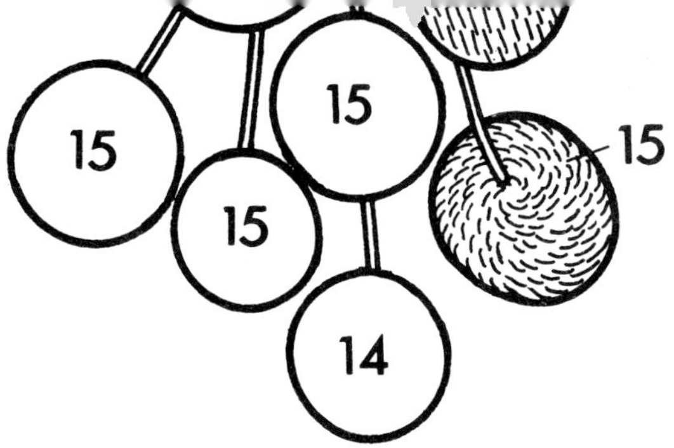

12 Cherries

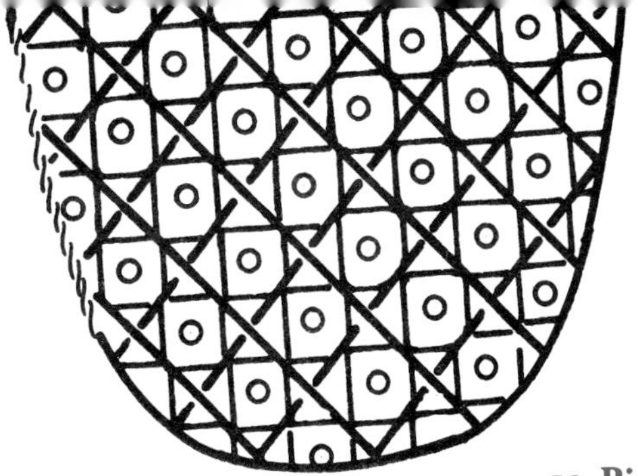

13 Pineapple

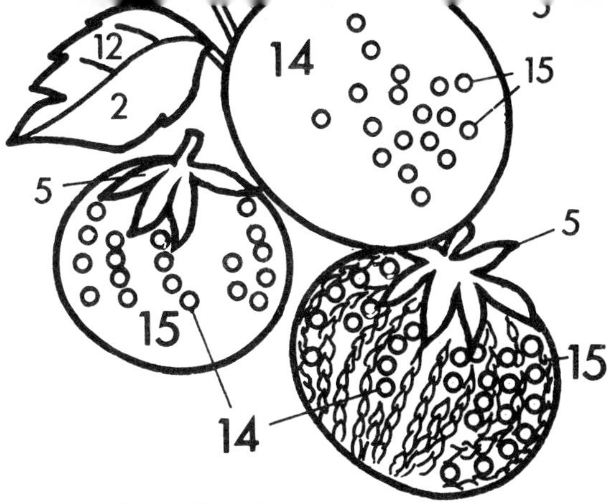

14 Strawberries

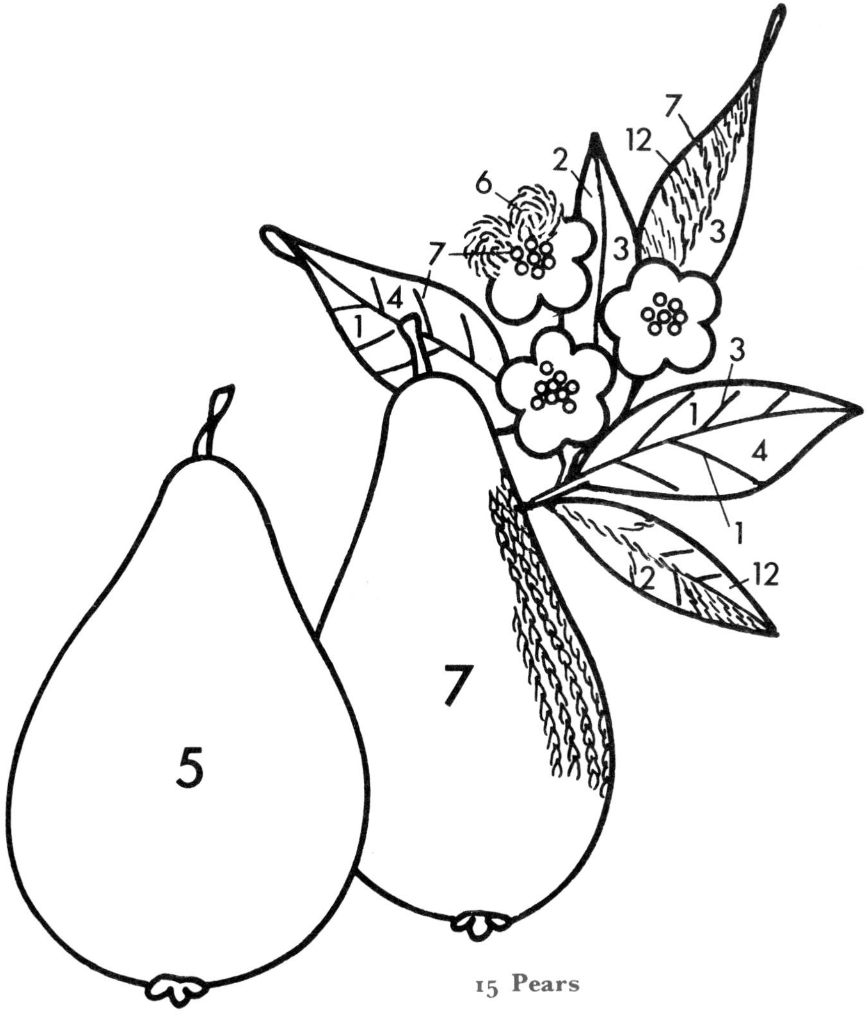

15 Pears

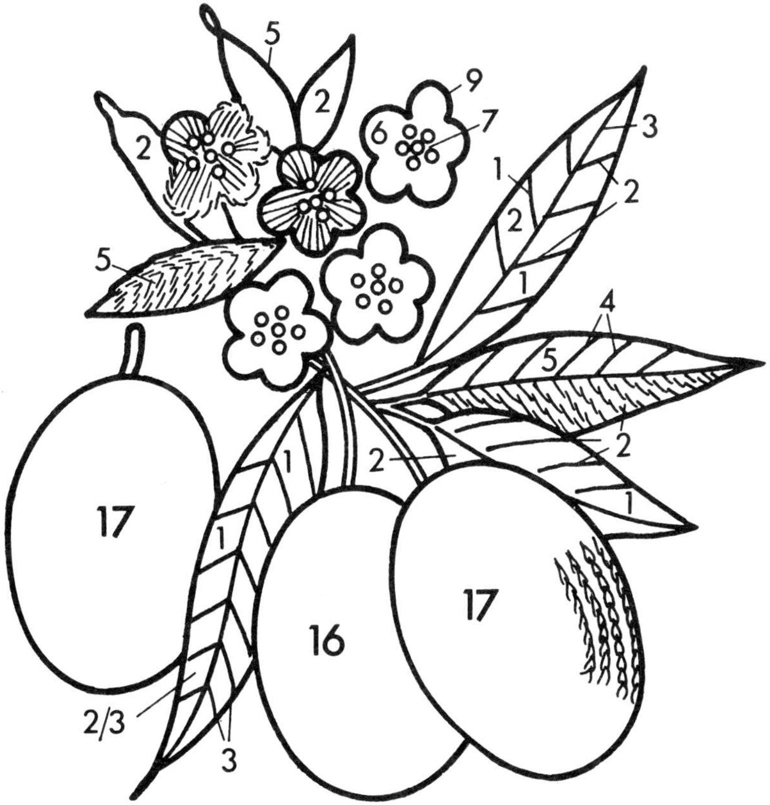

16 Plums

17 *Rampant lion bedspread*

Finished measurement: About 70″ x 100″.
Fabric: Blue terry cloth about 72″ x 102″, or size required. Orange terry, 17″ x 14″. Yellow terry, 36″ x 9″. Blue cotton fringe, 2 yards. Rickrack: 3 yards blue, optional.
Thread: Matching blue sewing thread.
Stitch: Machine zigzag, running chain.

A washable bedspread to delight a child. Test the fabric for dye fastness before making. If the color runs, rinse all the pieces in cool water to disperse the surplus dye.
Enlarge the outline opposite and cut paper shapes. Follow the cutting layout and cut the fabric pieces. Pin and baste the lion shapes into position on the bedspread. The dotted line shows where one fabric fits under another. Machine stitch into position. Pin and stitch the fringe into place. Embroider or machine stitch the eyes, nose and mouth. Turn up the hem as shown on page 123. Outline body with rickrack if required.

18 *Wild flower cushion*

Finished measurement: 9″ x 9″.
Fabric: White linen. Two squares 11″ x 11″.
Threads: D.M.C. 6-strand floss, one skein of each color. **1.** 307 buttercup; **2.** 605 light magenta; **3.** 604 magenta; **4.** 603 mid-magenta; **5.** 602 magenta; **6.** 601 magenta; **7.** 600 deep magenta; **8.** 351 geranium; **9.** 310 black; **10.** 472 parrot green; **11.** 469 deep parrot green; **12.** 794 light periwinkle; **13.** 793 mid-periwinkle; **14.** 792 deep periwinkle; **15.** 208 violet. Use three strands in the needle for numbers **1, 8, 10, 11, 12, 13, 14, 15.** Two strands for **2, 3, 4, 5, 6, 7.** One for **9.**
Needles: Crewel, No. 6 and 7.
Stitches: Satin, French knots, stem.

Trace the design onto the fabric, following the directions on page 121. The embroidery stitches are worked in the direction indicated in the diagram. Blend the colors in the bluebells as indicated, working a needleful of each color in turn. The stem stitch on the pink flower is worked in a circle around the flower center. Press and make up as shown on page 124.

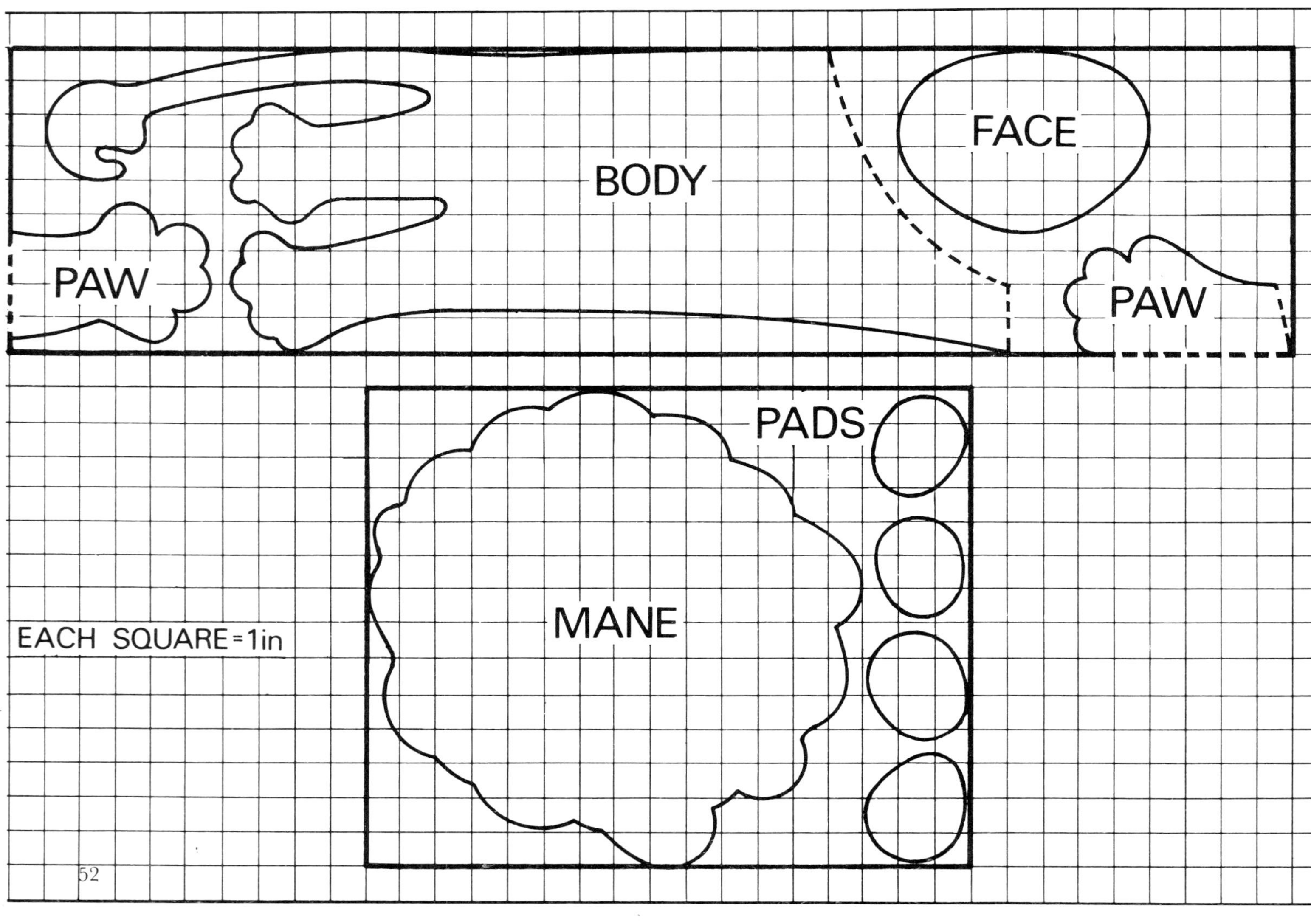

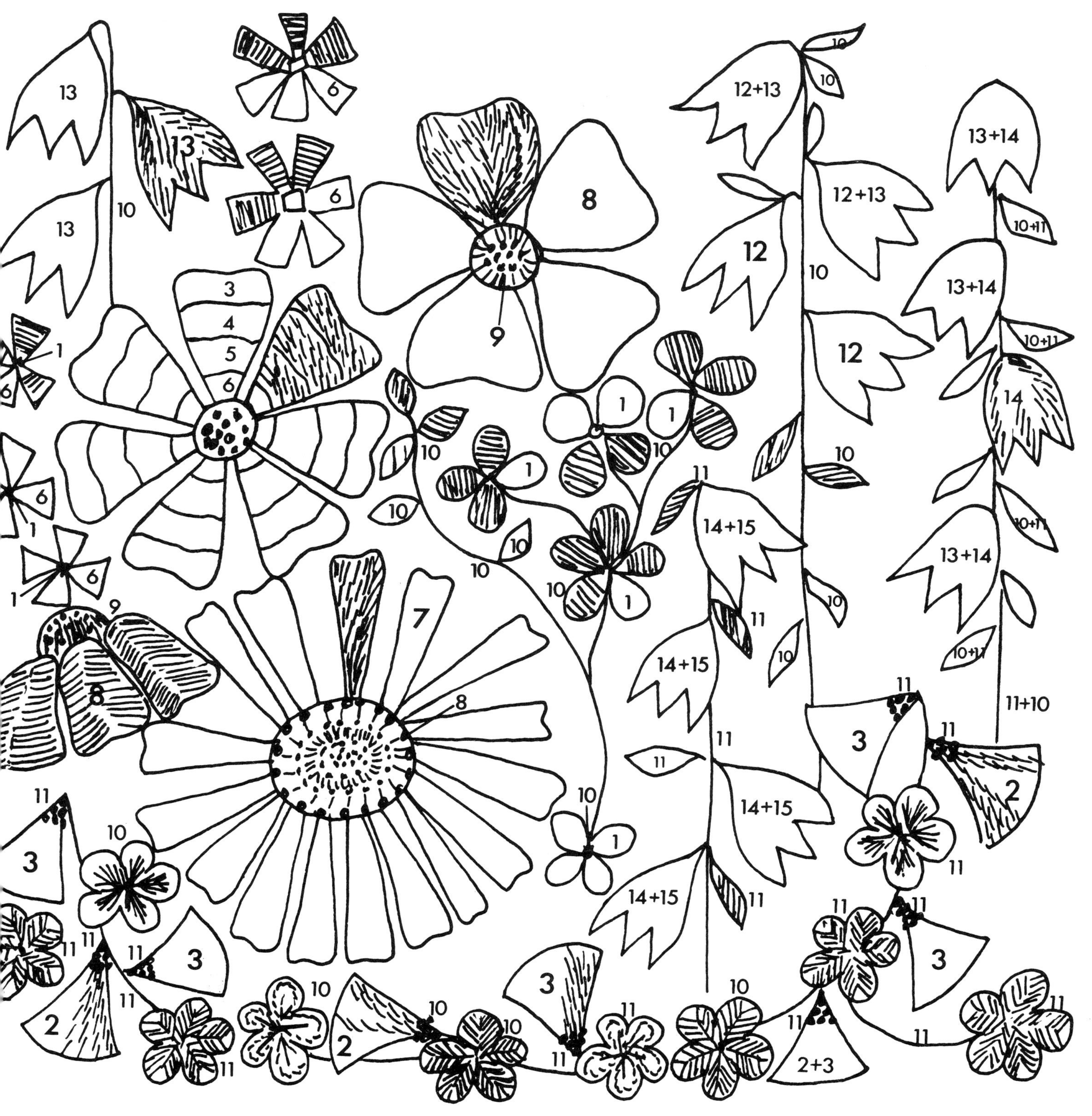

19-30

Signs of the Zodiac

19 Aries (March 21 – April 20)

20 Taurus (April 21 – May 21)

21 Gemini (May 22 – June 22)

22 Cancer (June 23 – July 23)

23 Leo (July 24 – August 23)

24 Virgo (August 24 – September 23)

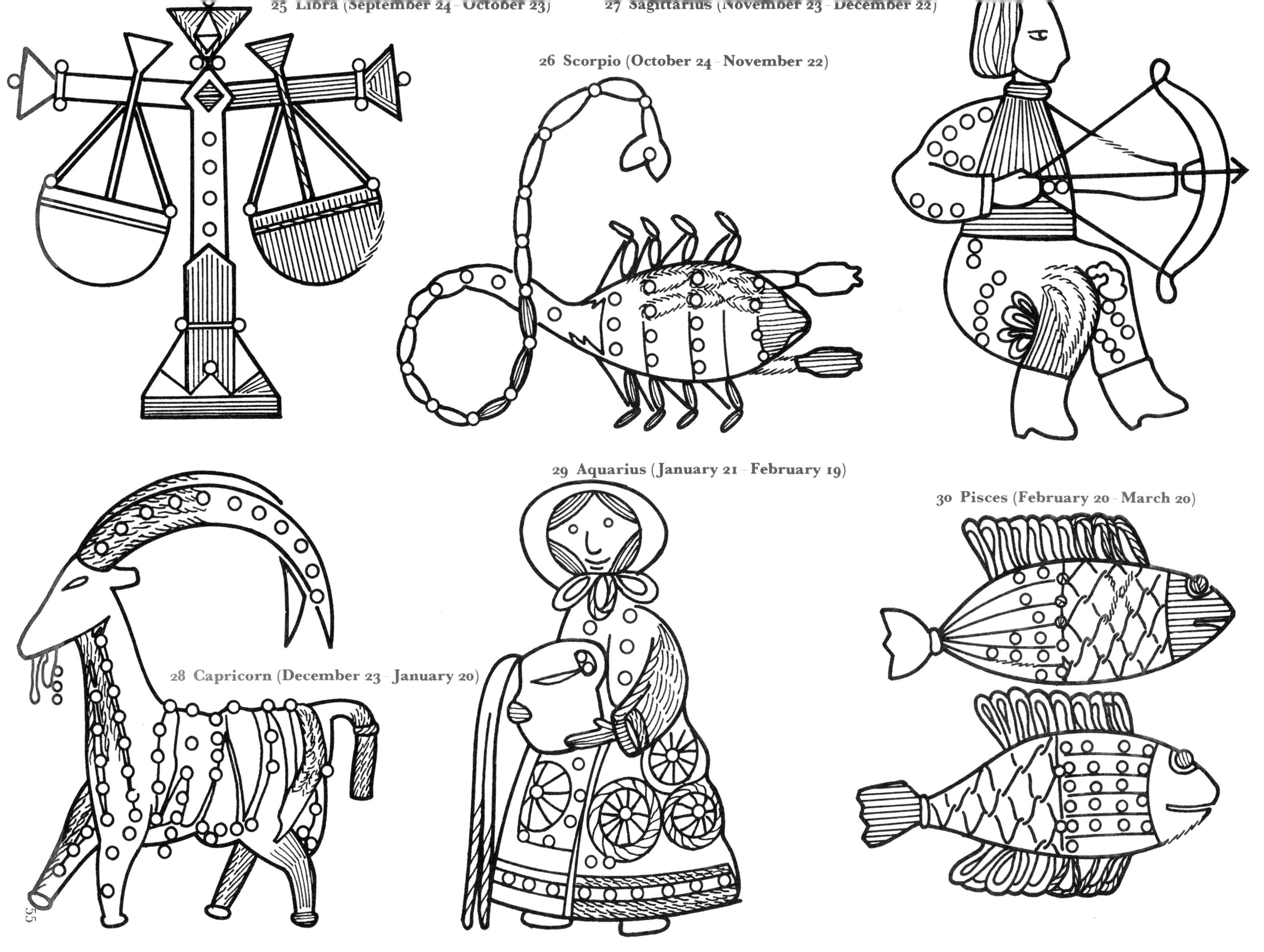

25 Libra (September 24 – October 23)

26 Scorpio (October 24 – November 22)

27 Sagittarius (November 23 – December 22)

28 Capricorn (December 23 – January 20)

29 Aquarius (January 21 – February 19)

30 Pisces (February 20 – March 20)

Here are five suggestions of ways in which the zodiac can be used to brighten gifts and clothes, but the possibilities are endless.

32-33

Hungarian panels

Finished measurement: Each motif about 5½″ square.
Fabric: Cream wool or linen, two 7″ squares.
Threads: D.M.C. Tapestry yarn, one skein of each color. **1.** 7605 pale rose; **2.** 7804 mid-rose; **3.** 7602 deep rose; **4.** 7437 orange; **5.** 7726 yellow; **6.** 7727 pale yellow; **7.** 7549 pale green; **8.** 7318 blue; **9.** 7850 red; **10.** 7768 green; **11.** 7364 olive green.
Needles: Chenille, No. 18.
Stitches: Detached chain, satin, French knots, stem.

Transfer the designs to the fabric as shown on page 121. Mount the fabric in a frame for ease of working the satin stitch. On the round flower motif, work the stem stitch circle after the petals are complete.
Prepare for framing as shown on page 122.

34

Pimpernel rose

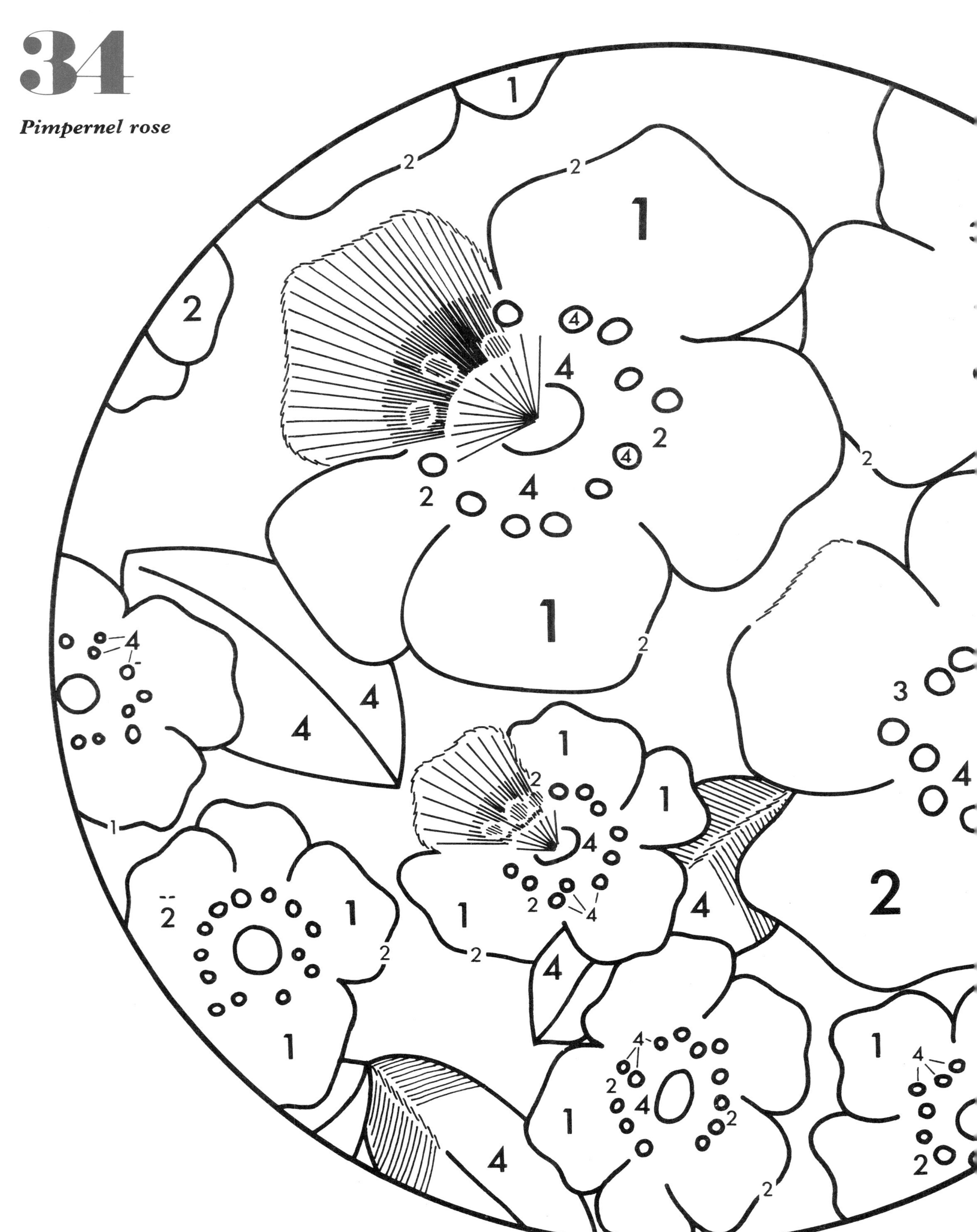

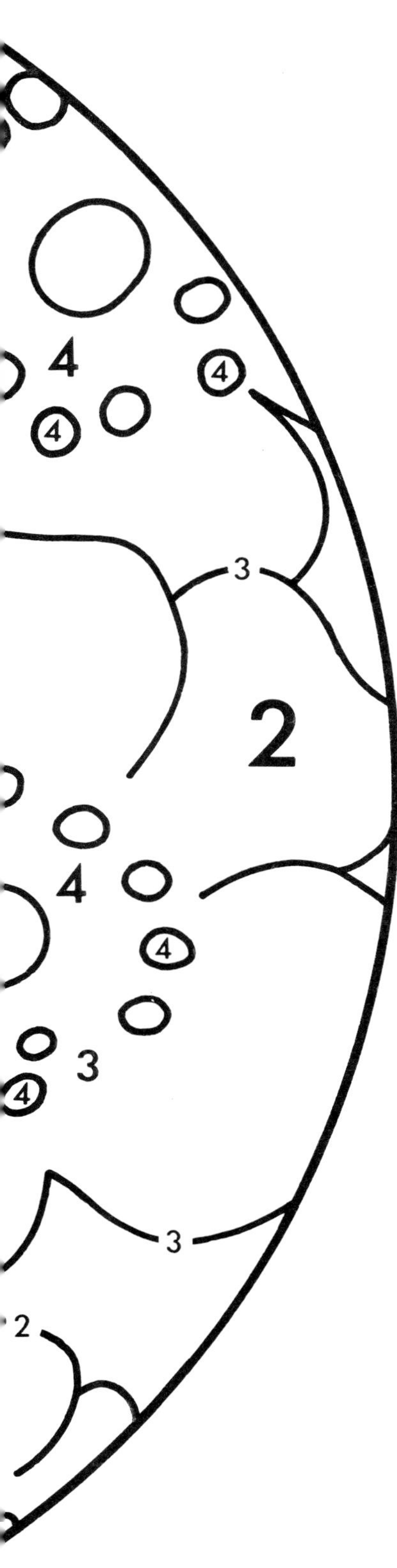

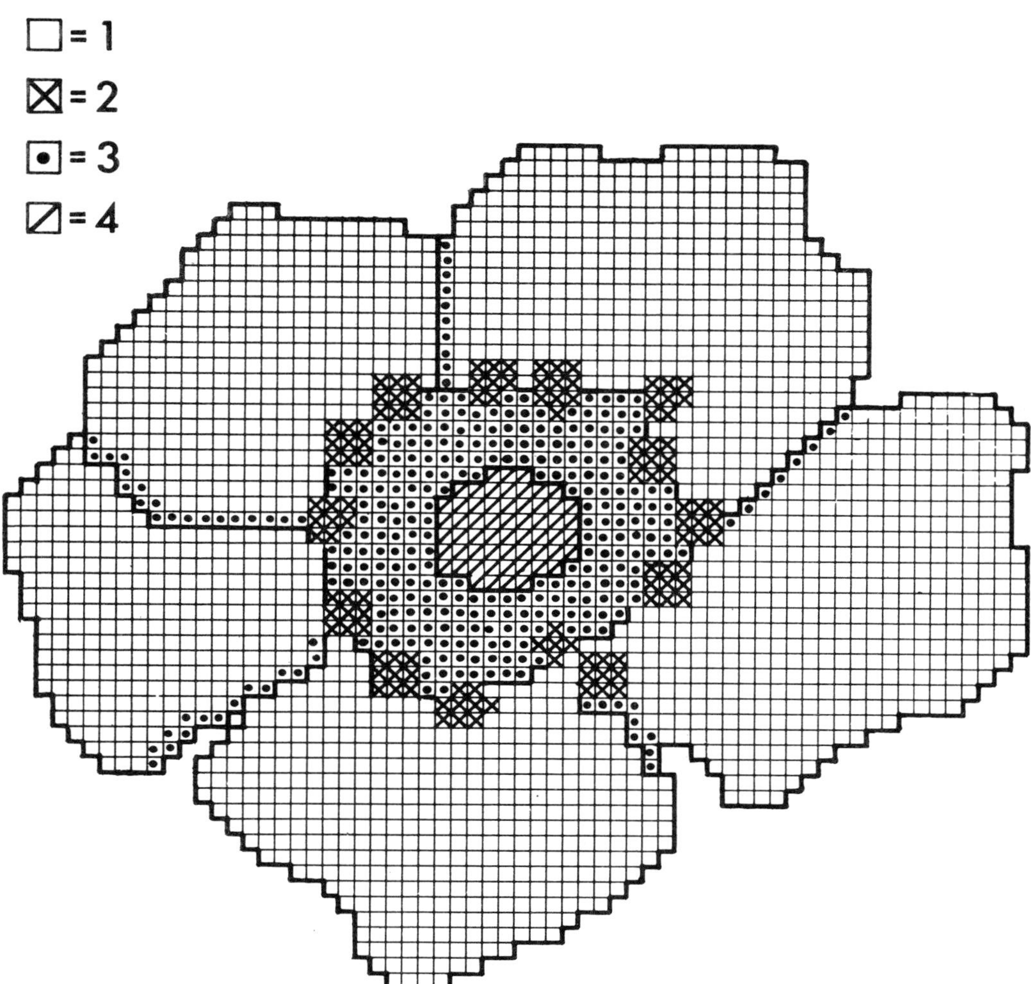

35,36

Wild rose pillow and floral alphabet (next page)

Finished measurement: About 10″ diameter.
Fabric: Bright pink dress linen with an easily counted weave, 18 to 20 threads to the inch. Two 12″ squares.
Threads: D.M.C. 6-strand floss; 3 skeins 725 amber gold; 1 skein white; 1 skein 3348 bright green; 1 skein 998 grass green.
Needles: Tapestry 22 or 24.
Stitch: Cross-stitch.

Overcast the edges of one of the squares of fabric and baste center lines. The number of strands of floss needed to work the design will depend on the weight of fabric. Try a few stitches in a corner. Three strands have been used here. The stitches should cover the ground well. Work from the chart taking the cross-stitches over two threads of fabric. Make up as shown on page 124.

Floral alphabet

35, 36

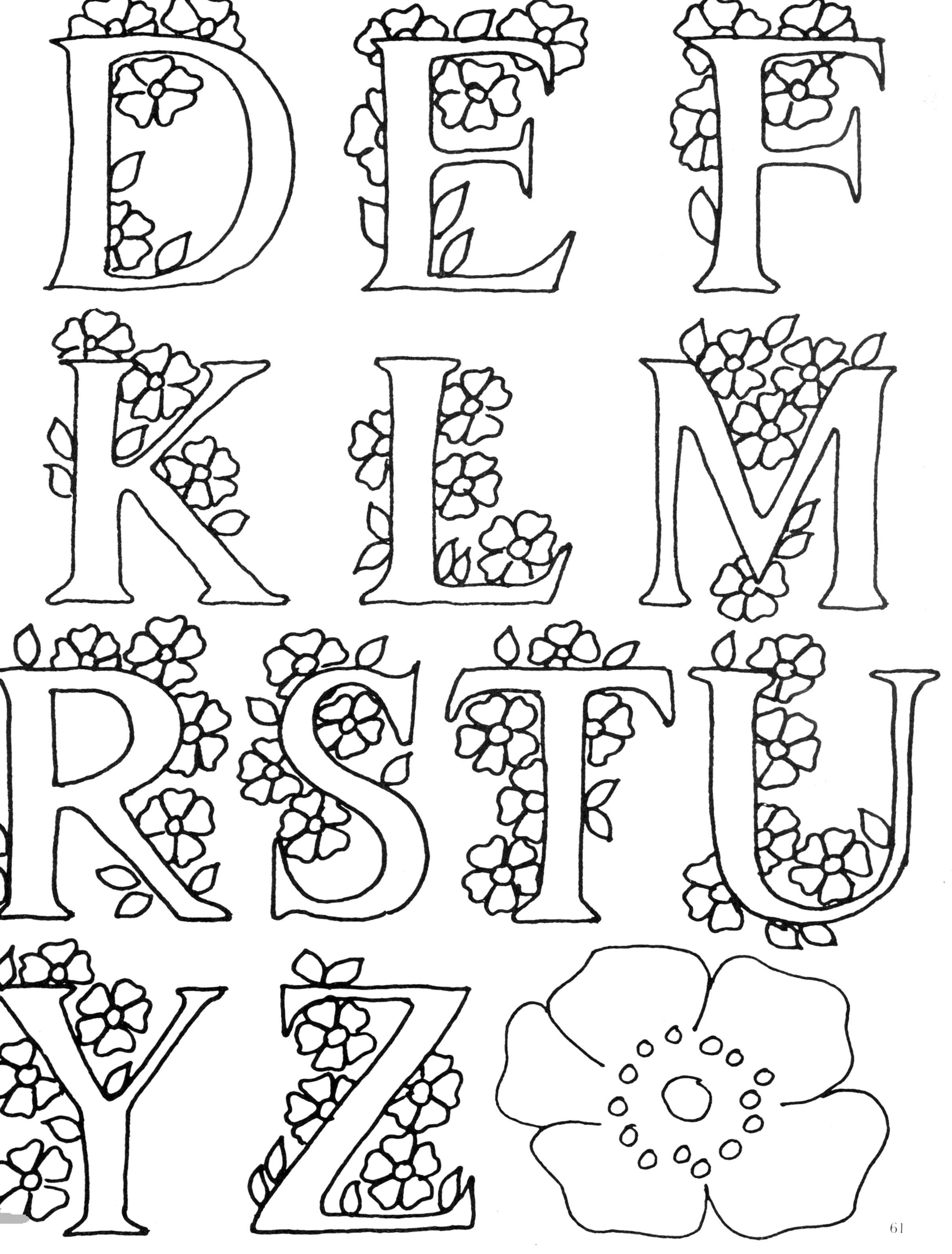
D E F
K L M
R S T U
Y Z

37-48

Pick your favorite plant

Flower measurement: Not larger than 4″ x 3½″.
Fabric: White linen.
Threads: D.M.C. 6-strand floss, one skein of each color.
Needles: Crewel, No. 7.
Stitches: Chain, detached chain, satin, stem, French knots.

Add a personal touch to small gifts with these quickly worked flower motifs. Transfer the design as shown on page 121. Follow the illustrations for color and the diagram for direction of stitch. Use two threads of the floss.

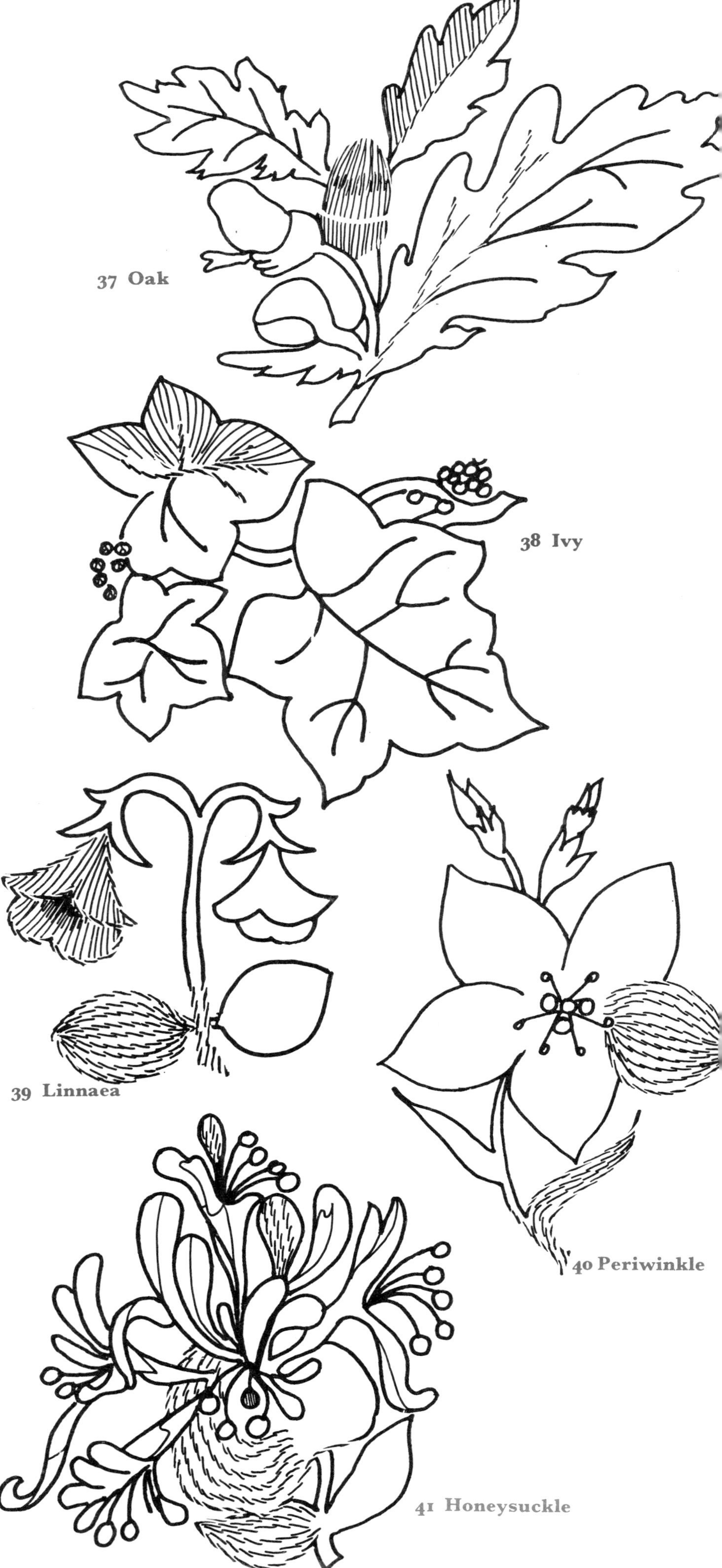

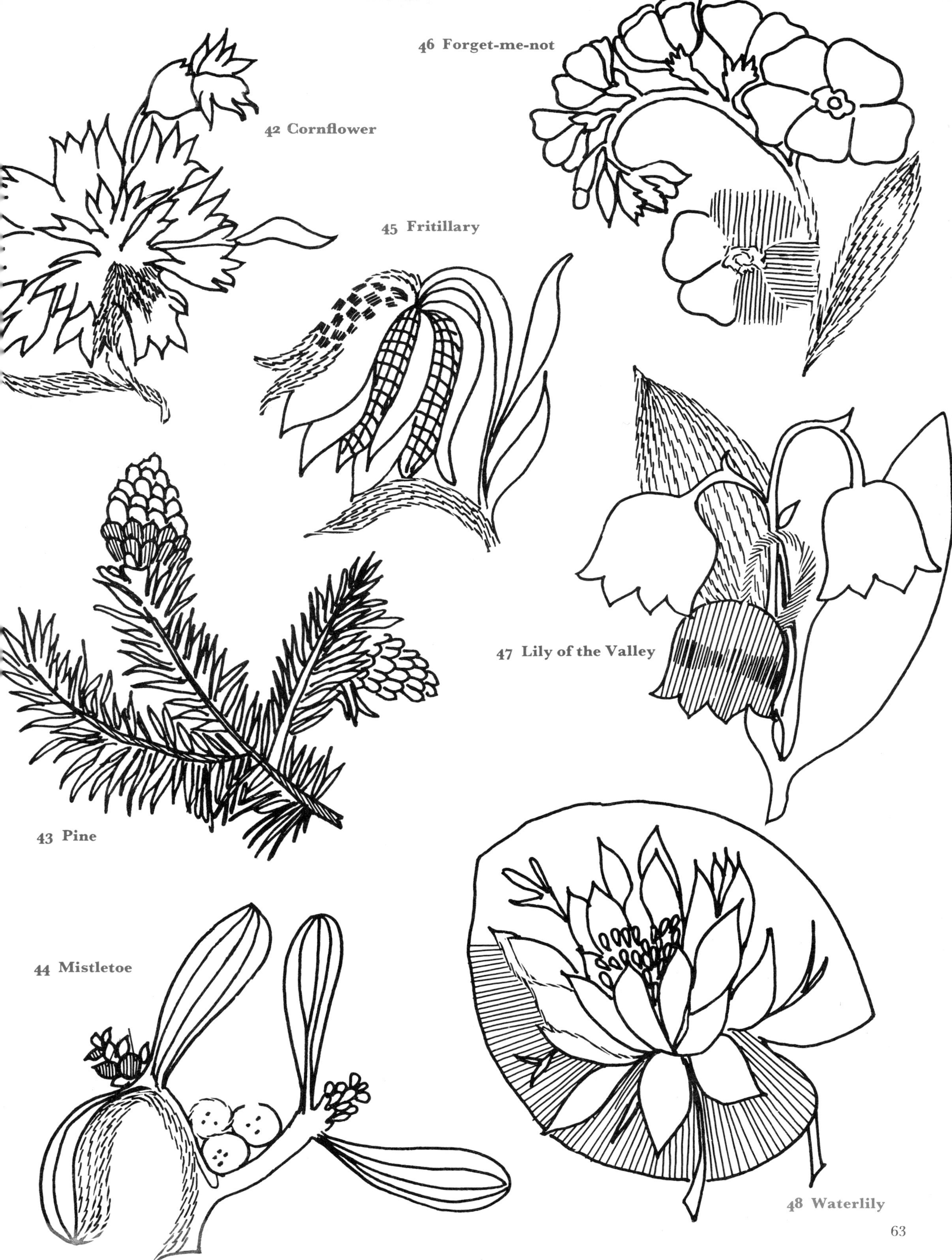
46 Forget-me-not
42 Cornflower
45 Fritillary
47 Lily of the Valley
43 Pine
44 Mistletoe
48 Waterlily

White anemone footstool

Finished measurement: About $17'' \times 11\frac{1}{2}''$ – area shown on chart.
Fabric: Single canvas 20 threads to the inch. For measuring a stool for the required canvas, see page 123.
Threads: Bucilla Crewel Wool. **1.** 8 cards 1 white; **2.** 2 cards 27 light olive; **3.** 3 cards 28 medium olive; **4.** 1 card 74 lime twist; **5.** Background, 12 cards 29 dark olive. Use 2 strands in the needle.
Needles: Tapestry, No. 20.
Stitch: Cross-stitch. Work over two threads of the canvas.

For a footstool with a side drop, extend the background to the size desired. Leave the corner areas unworked as shown on page 123. Mark the center lines of the canvas both vertically and horizontally. Count and mark with basting lines the extent of the chart. Each square represents one stitch. Begin at one side and work across the chart, completing each row of pattern and background. Add texture interest by working larger cross-stitches over four threads toward the center of the flowers. Block and make up as shown on pages 122, 123.
The pillow is shown with the design repeated twice, or you can use the design exactly as shown on the footstool.

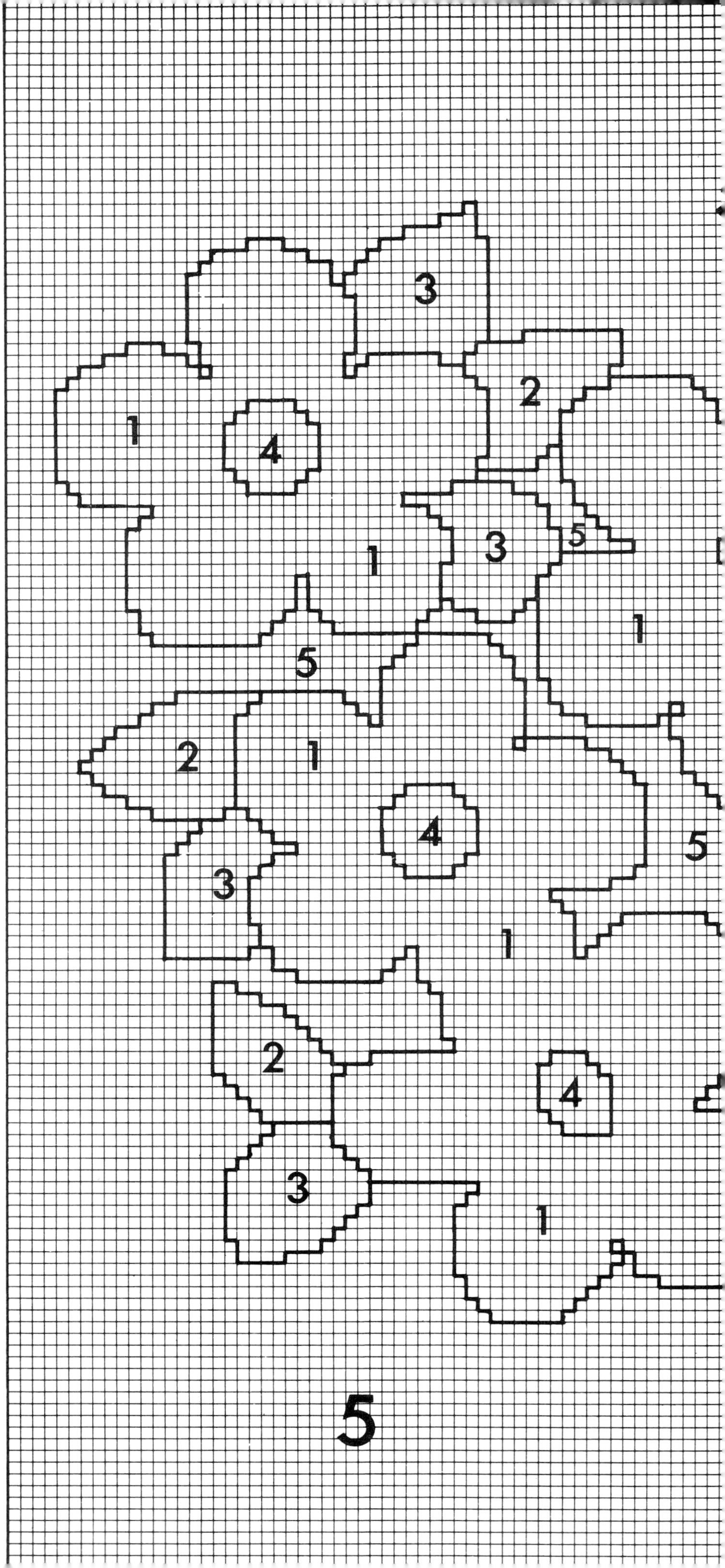

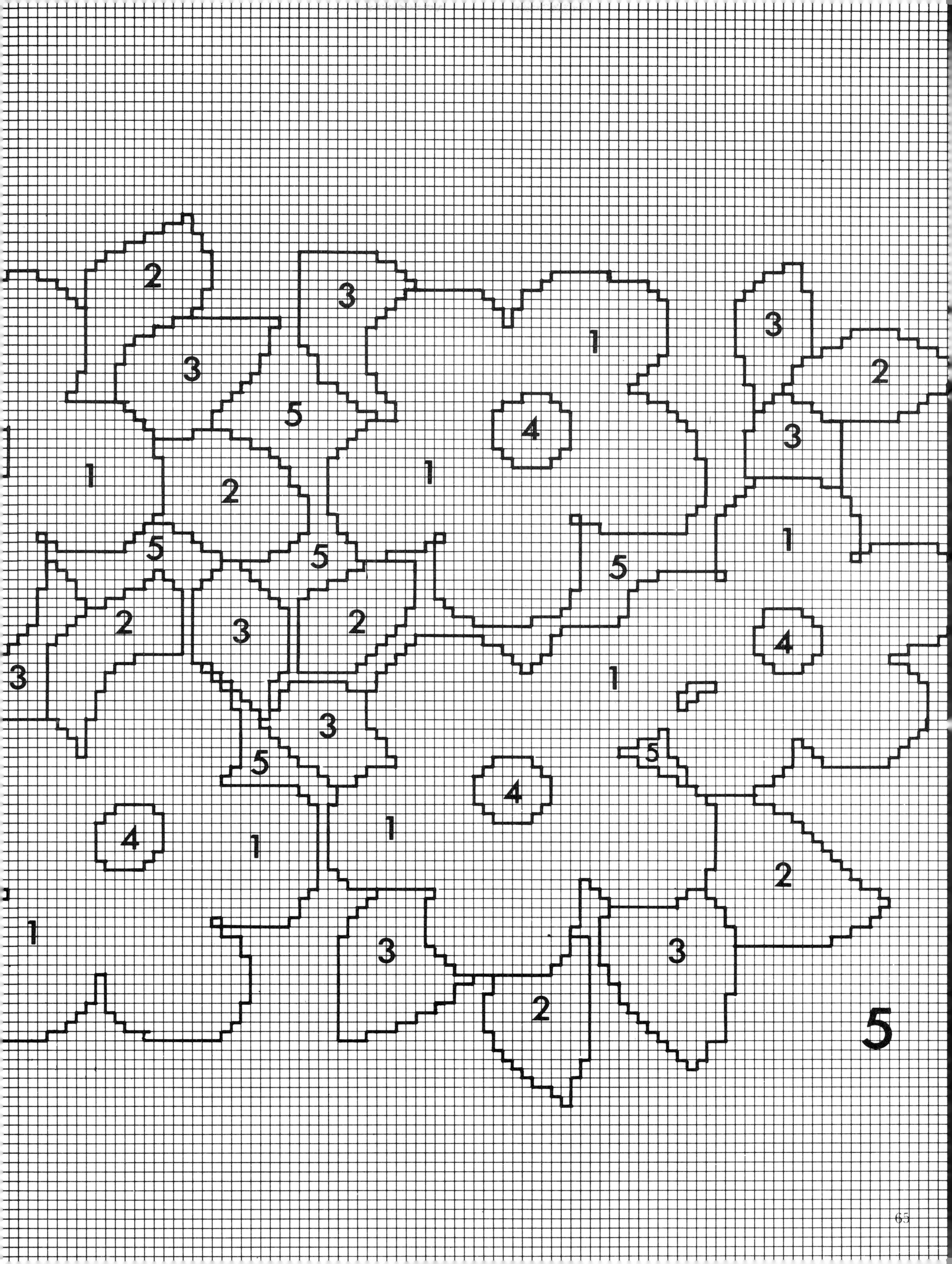
5

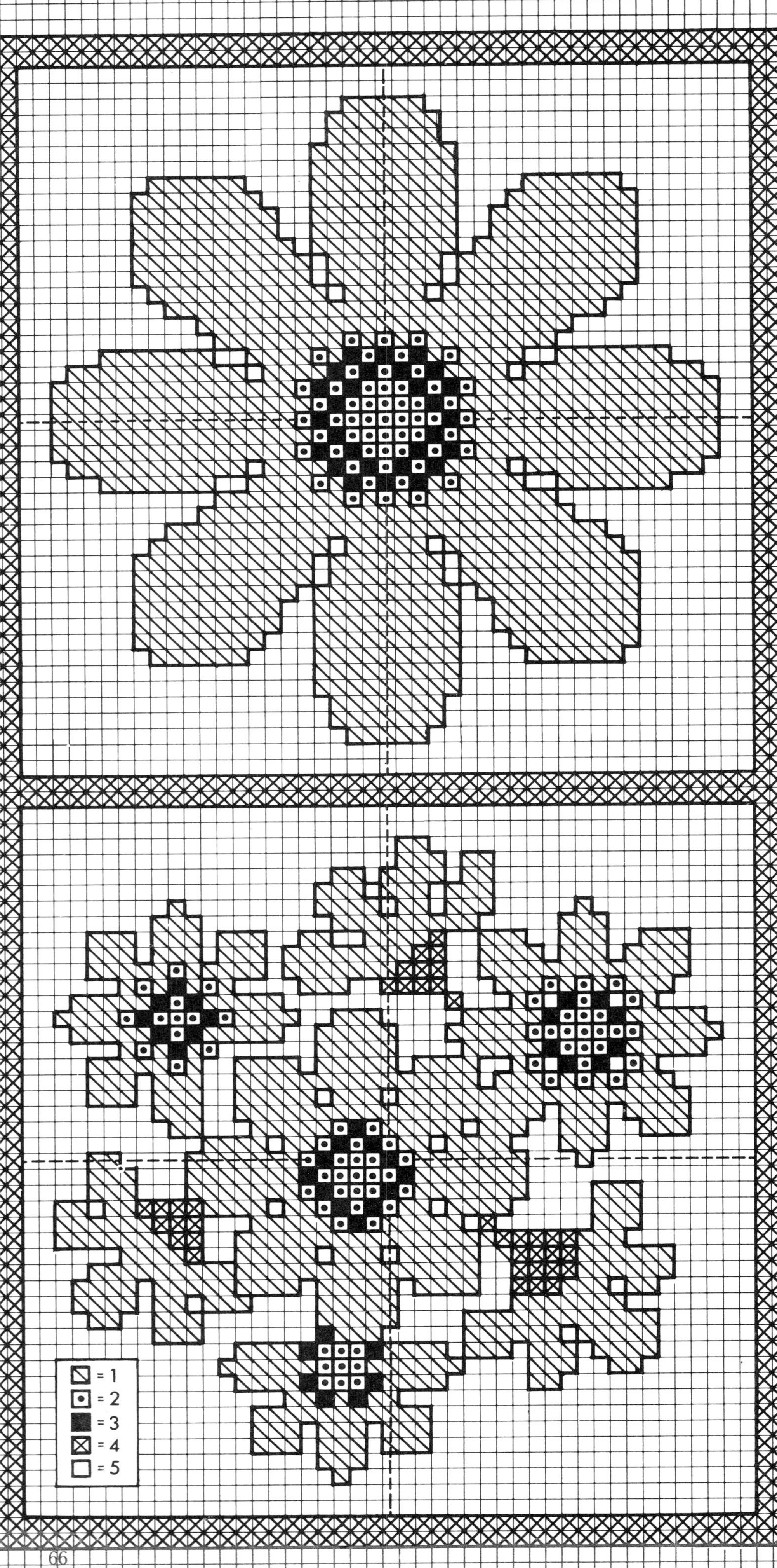

50 *Daisy rug*

Finished measurement: About 36″ x 47½″.
Fabric: 1½ yards of 36″ wide canvas with 4 stitches to the inch.
Threads: Columbia-Minerva Rug yarn. Number of 1¾ oz skeins in parentheses. **1.** 2 off-white (16); **2.** 5 bright yellow (3); **3.** 12 medium gold (2); **4.** 26 Kelly green (13); **5.** 27 forrest green (35).
Needles: Rug.
Stitches: Cross-stitch. Check the method for the stitch from the diagram on page126.

Mark the centers of the canvas. Count the number of stitches out from the center and work from the chart. Each square represents one stitch. Work straight across in rows, stitching the background and pattern together. Keep the needles threaded with five colors. On reaching the end of one color, count the stitches and bring to the front where it is next needed. Work in the new color which will automatically cover the long strand at the back. Block as on page 122, and herringbone stitch the hem into position on the reverse side.

Blue town 51

(Graph pattern)

Each square=1ir

Mexican daisy place mat 52

Finished measurement: 17½″ x 13½″.
Fabric: White linen, 18½″ x 14½″.
Threads: D.M.C. 6-strand floss, two skeins of each color. **1.** 941 orange; **2.** 552 petunia; **3.** 815 raspberry.
Needles: Crewel, No. 6.
Stitches: Rumanian, stem.

Trace the flower and the required initial onto the fabric as shown on page 121. Using four strands in the needle, work the petals in Rumanian stitch. With three strands, work the circles and initial in stem stitch. Work three rows of chain stitch around the hemline of the mat, one in each of the three colors. Press and make up as shown on page 122.

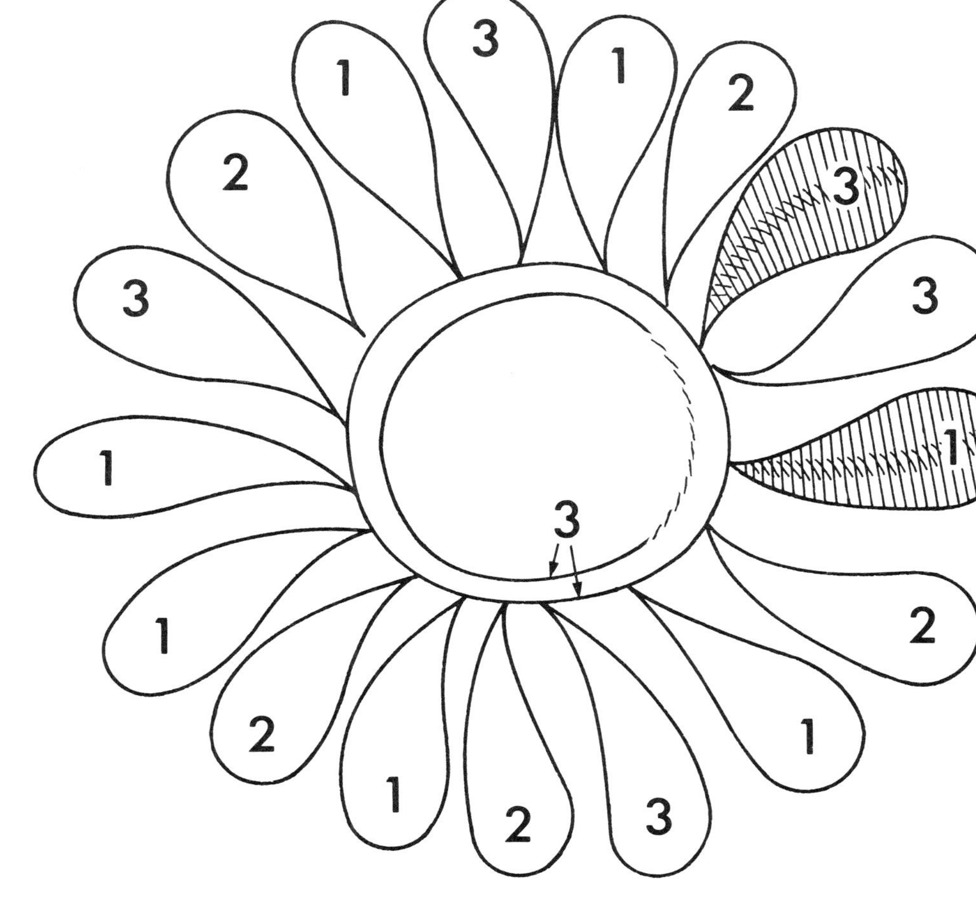

Mexican daisy panel 53

Finished measurement: About 5½″ square.
Fabric: Orange linen, 7″ square.
Threads: D.M.C. 6-strand floss, one skein of each. **1.** 712 cream; **2.** 743 golden yellow; **3.** 947 orange; **4.** 602 magenta; **5.** 552 mauve. Use four strands in the needle.
Needles: Crewel, No. 6.
Stitches: Stem.
Small and large sequins.

Trace the design onto the fabric as shown on page 121. Fill the petals with stem stitch as shown in the diagram. Work a French knot to hold the center sequins in place. Stitch the large sequins through the ready-made holes. Work rows of stem stitch closely around the sequins. Press and prepare for framing as shown on page 122.

Mexican laced belt

Finished measurement: Approximately $3\frac{1}{4}''$ deep. Length to own measurement.
Fabric: Orange dress linen, $4\frac{1}{2}''$ deep and length to own measurement.
Threads: Bucilla Crewel Wool. **1.** 17 coppertone (3 cards); **2.** 1 white (1); **3.** 3 dark yellow (1); **4.** 86 fuchsia (2); **5.** 33 royal blue (1).
Needles: Chenille, No. 22.
Stitches: Satin, French knots.
Sequins for the flower centers.

Onto a waist-length strip of tissue paper, $4\frac{1}{2}''$ deep, trace the repeating flower motifs. As shown in the photograph, rotate the color sequence for each succeeding flower by $\frac{1}{3}$. Baste the design and prepare the fabric as explained on page 121. With two strands of yarn, embroider the petals in satin stitch. Start with the dark blue petal and keep to the same sequence throughout. Attach the sequins in the center circles, holding them in place with a French knot. Press and make up as shown on page 122.

Mexican glasses case

Finished measurement: $7\frac{1}{4}''$ x $3\frac{1}{2}''$.
Fabric: Orange dress linen, two pieces $8\frac{1}{2}''$ x $5''$.
Threads: Appleton's Crewel Wool, one skein of each color. **1.** 766 biscuit brown; **2.** 452 mauve; **3.** 946 rose pink.
Needles: Chenille, No. 22.
Stitches: Satin, French knots.
Sequins for the flower centers.
Transfer the design to the fabric as described on page 121. With two strands of crewel wool, work satin stitch as indicated in the diagram. Stem stitch is closely worked around the circles and the sequins are held in place with a French knot. Press and make up as shown on page 122.

56

Footstool and pillow

Fabric: Fine wool or weave linen.
Threads: Appleton's Tapestry yarn, two skeins each of numbers 1 and 10, one skein each of the remainder. **1.** 991 white; **2.** 943 pale bright rose pink; **3.** 438 leaf green; **4.** 253 grass green; **5.** 353 light gray green; **6.** 355 dark gray green; **7.** 243 light olive green; **8.** 542 early English green; **9.** 403 light sea green; **10.** 406 dark sea green; **11.** 752 pale rose; **12.** 946 deep bright rose pink; **13.** 501a scarlet; **14.** 755 mid rose pink; **15.** 144 dull rose pink.
Needles: Tapestry or Crewel.
Stitches: Long and short, satin.

Trace the design onto the fabric using the enlarging technique described on page 121. For ease of working mount the fabric in a frame. With the appropriate number of strands in the needle, work the leaves in long and short stitch and the flowers in satin stitch. Press and make up as shown on pages 122, 123.

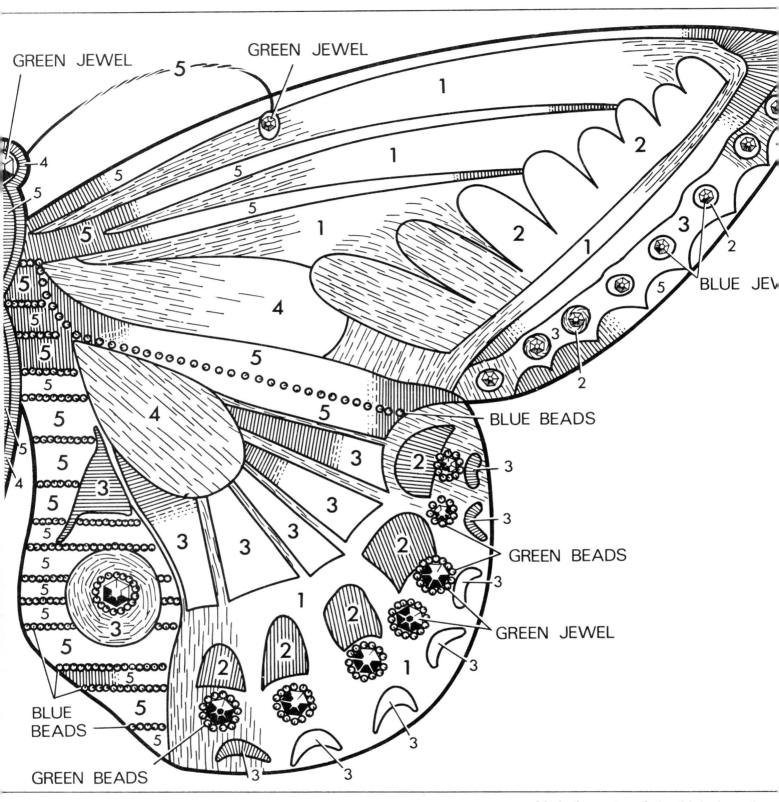

GREEN JEWEL

BLUE JEWELS

BLUE BEADS

GREEN BEADS

Finished measurement: About 21″ × $10\frac{1}{2}$″
Fabric: White linen 24″ wide by $13\frac{1}{2}$″ deep. White cardboard 21″ wide by $10\frac{1}{2}$″ deep. Fabric adhesive. Blue and green beads. Small blue and large green glass "jewels."
Threads: D.M.C. 6-strand floss, 3 skeins of each color and 4 of No. 5. **1.** 798 cobalt blue; **2.** 806 peacock blue; **3.** 797 azure; **4.** 906 parrot green; **5.** 500 grass green.
Needles: Crewel, No. 6. Beading needle.
Stitches: Satin, split.

Mark the center of the fabric in each direction. Transfer the design as shown on page 121. Use four strands of floss in the needle, and following the directions indicated in the outline drawing, work in a free manner. For the background areas of the patterned wings, work split stitch in open rows. Work the satin stitch blocks so that they slightly overlap the split stitch areas. Stitch the jewels in position and surround with beads. Fasten the beads upright with a stitch at each side.

More beautiful patterns

59

Hedgerow, a freely stitched design that doubles as an elegant pillow and a matching framed picture. *Tracing pattern on page 105.*

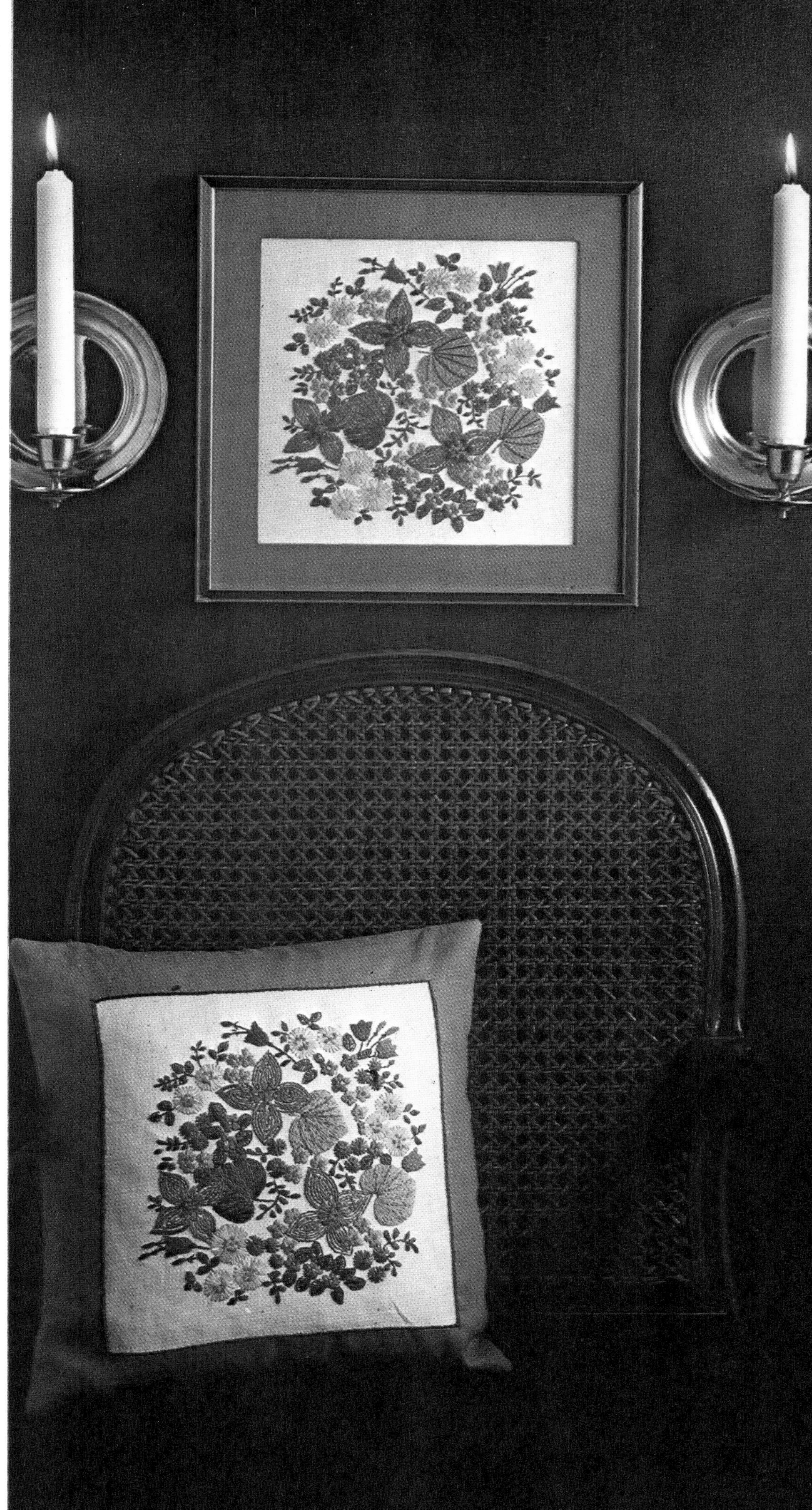

60

A charming yellow rose design in needlepoint for a pair of slippers.

Finished measurement: The slippers may be made to fit any size foot by extending the tapered ends, but cut out the shape on paper before starting to check the fit of the upper.
Fabric: Double canvas, 10 holes to the inch, 26″ x 13″. Corduroy for lining, half yard, 36″ wide. Piece of leather "split" or a piece of chamois for the soles. One pair cork soles to foot size. Stiff cardboard, 12″ × 12″. Embroidery frame.
Threads: Appleton's Crewel yarn. Three skeins 761 for the background, one skein each of the following: dull china blue range: 927, 925, 922; brown olive range: 313, 315; early English green range: 542, 544, 546; bright yellow: 552, 554; golden brown: 905; gray green: 352.
Needles: Tapestry needle No. 20. Crewel needle No. 7.
Mark out the two slipper upper shapes on the canvas, leaving space between them for making up. Mount the canvas in the frame. Mark the center of each shape and work the design outward. Block the embroidery as shown on page 122 and cut out the uppers, leaving an inch of canvas all around. Using the cork insoles as a pattern, cut out two more soles from the cardboard. Still using the cork insoles as a pattern, cut out the shape for each foot in the chamois and then in the corduroy, leaving an extra inch all around. Cover the cardboard sole shapes with the chamois, lacing on the reverse side (see illustration). Cover the cork insoles with corduroy and lace in the same way. Use the embroidered upper as a guide and cut out the corduroy linings and line the embroidered upper. Run a gathering thread $\frac{1}{8}$ inch in from the embroidery edging and, drawing it up, try the uppers on, easing the gathers to fit the foot. Place the foot on the sole covered with corduroy and try the uppers again, turning the 1 inch of canvas to the underside of the insole. Pin and then stitch the uppers firmly to the insole. Glue the insole to the sole, wrong sides facing, using a fabric glue.

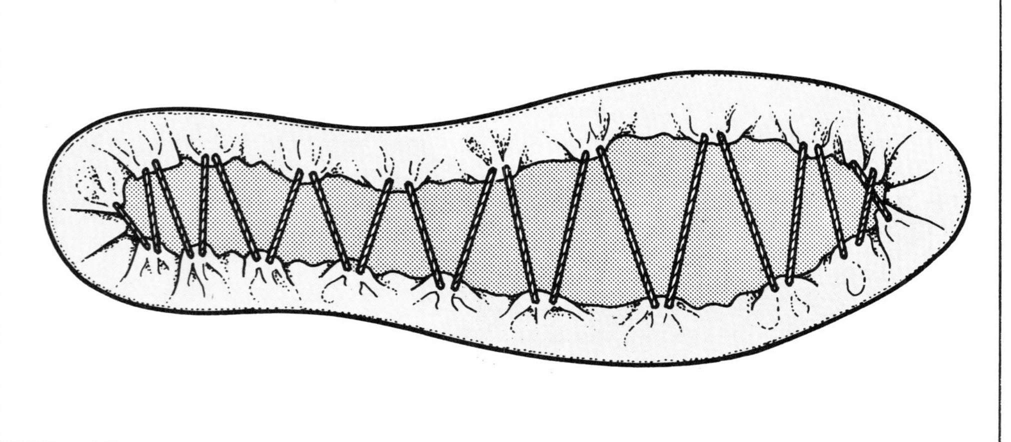

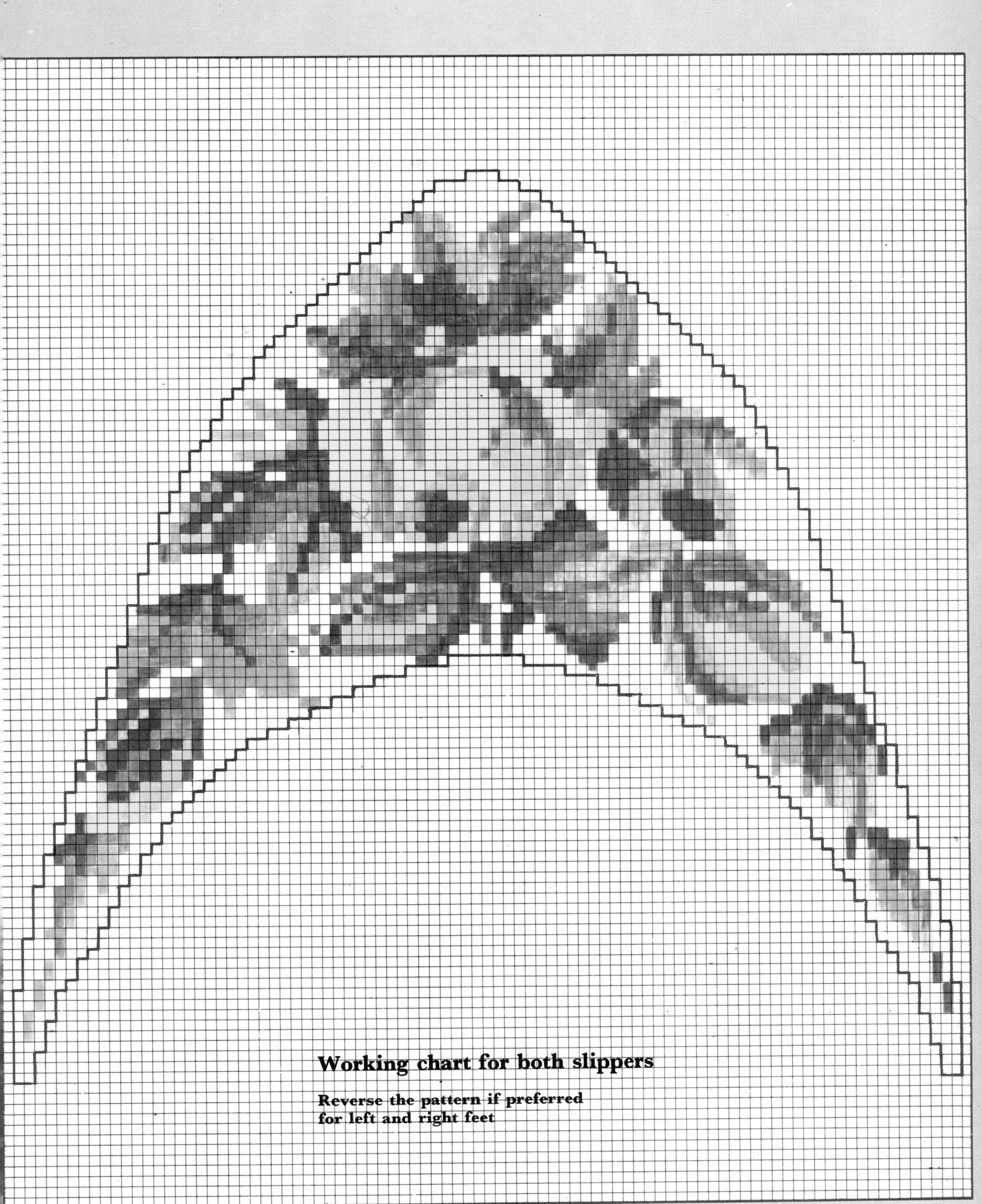

Working chart for both slippers

Reverse the pattern if preferred for left and right feet

61

A cross-stitch handbag, made by inserting an embroidered panel into a linen bag.

Finished measurement: About 11" x 8".
Fabric: Canvas 16 threads to the inch, 12" x 9". Dark brown linen 24" x 18". An equivalent amount of lining and interlining.
Threads: D.M.C. Tapestry yarn. To work the front flap, **1.** 5 skeins 7602 pink; **2.** 2 skeins white; **3.** 3 skeins black; **4.** 3 skeins 7467 brown.
Needles: Tapestry, No. 18.
Stitches: Cross-stitch.

A handbag to complement a knitted suit. A cross-stitch panel is set into the front flap of a brown linen handbag. The handle extends to form a gusset. The repeating pattern of the embroidery is easily adapted to fit the size of bag you prefer.
Mark the center lines of the canvas. Match one of the motifs to the center line of the canvas. Work the cross-stitch over two threads to within 2" of the edge of the canvas.
Make up as shown on page 124 .

62

Cross-stitch butterfly motif.

Finished measurement: 5" x 5½".
Fabric: Blouse made from a bought pattern, or a ready-made blouse. ¼ yard soft, open linen.
Thread: D.M.C. 6-strand floss. 3 skeins 309 deep rose.
Needles: Tapestry, No. 22.
Stitch: Cross-stitch.

Cut a piece of linen about 6" x 6½". Mark the center. The embroidery is worked on the blouse front before making up. Pin and baste the linen into the required position. Using four strands of floss, work from the center of the butterfly. Stitch through both layers of fabric, working cross-stitch over the linen. When the butterfly is complete, withdraw the threads of linen leaving the stitches on the surface of the blouse fabric. Press. Complete the making up of the blouse as instructed in the bought pattern. For a ready-made blouse, work the embroidery in the same way. Be sure that the blouse front is as flat as possible before basting the linen in place.

63,64

These two symbolic kneelers represent the Holy Spirit (the dove) and the Redeemer (the vine).
See charts, below, and on the following pages.

Finished measurements: The tops of the kneelers illustrated are approximately 9″ × 12″ and the borders, between 1-1½″ deep, plus a 2-inch turning allowance, making the final canvas size that will be required, 16″ × 19″.
On the charts, each square represents one stitch, and the scale of your canvas, i.e. how many threads per inch, will determine the finished size of the design itself.
The following is an approximate guide:
10 threads per inch—finished size of design, 9″ × 12″.
14 threads per inch—finished size, 6¾″ × 8½″.
18 threads per inch—finished size, 5″ × 6¾″.
These kneeler designs have been planned so that they may be used both vertically and horizontally.

Materials and stitches: As embroidered kneelers receive hard wear and must last for many years, the stitches used must cover the canvas completely, be well-padded on the back, and be well-integrated with the canvas—tent stitch and rice stitch for example. For a beginner, the whole kneeler can be worked in a single stitch such as cross stitch, but in simple bold designs a variety of stitches can be worked to add textural interest, and for this kind of embroidery single thread canvas is best.

On coarse canvases (10-12 threads per inch) carpet thrums are quickly worked and are particularly hard wearing, but on finer canvases either tapestry wool or crewel wool would be more in scale. Carpet thrums have a limited color range, whereas the other wools present a much wider choice.
Find the center of the canvas and of the chart and mark both. Begin at the center of the design and work outward to insure that the motif is correctly placed on the canvas. Complete the top of the kneeler and leave two (on finer canvas, three) threads unworked before starting the border; when the embroidery is finished, block and stretch the canvas as shown on page 122. Make up as shown on page 125.

▲▼ *Border of the dove kneeler and working chart*

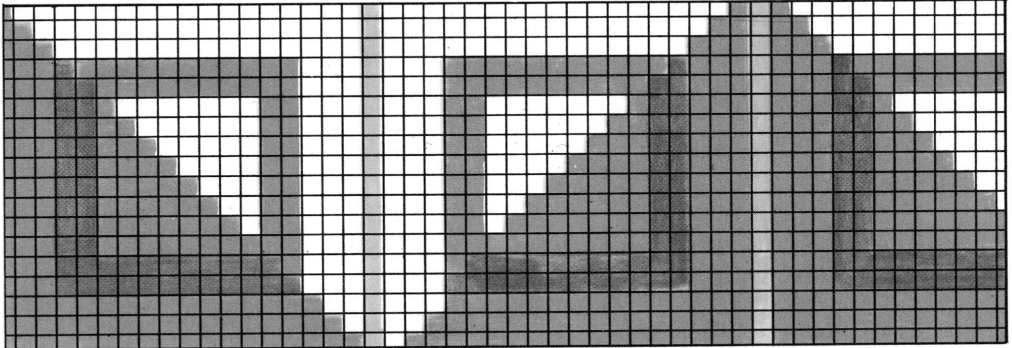

▼ *Border design which can be worked for either the grapes or dove kneeler*

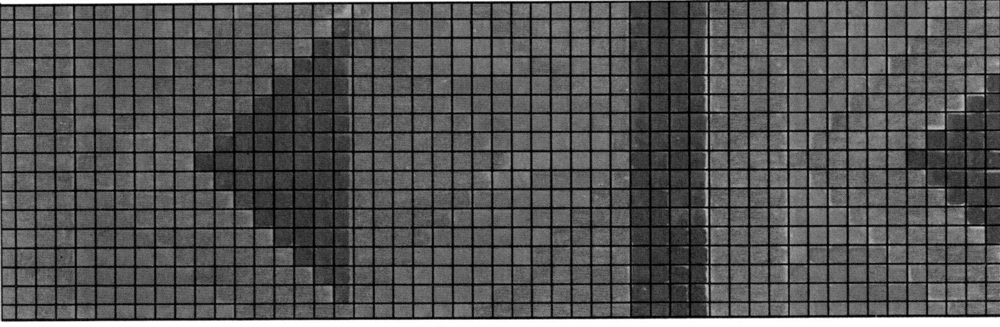

65

This striking tablecloth in blackwork would be equally attractive on a white or strongly contrasting background.
See chart on pages 106-107.

66

Two simple stitches achieve dramatic effect on this richly decorated table runner.
See chart on page 108.

67-71

The appeal of these five pillows depends largely on the use of strong clear colors to work the bold floral designs
Tracing patterns on pages 111-115

72

This colorful peony in shades of fuchsia, rose and pink is bordered by luxuriant green leaves. It makes a highly decorative pillow cover or elaborate framed picture.
Tracing patterns on pages 116-117.

73

The lively design of this summer handbag worked on coarse white linen is emphasized with clear, bright colours
Tracing pattern on pages 118-119.

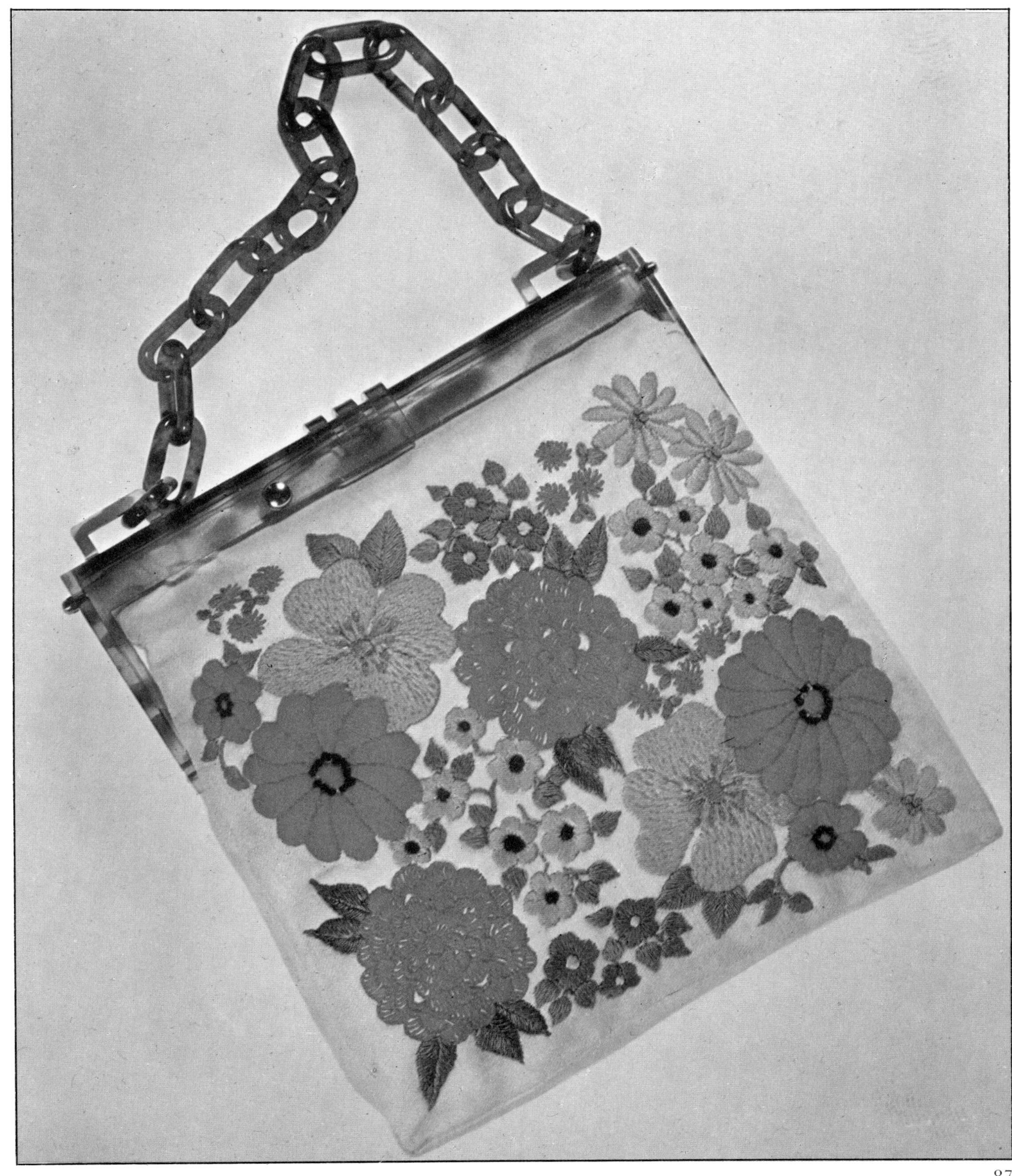

74

This delightful flowery appliqué bedspread lends itself to a variety of embroidery techniques.
Tracing design on page 120.

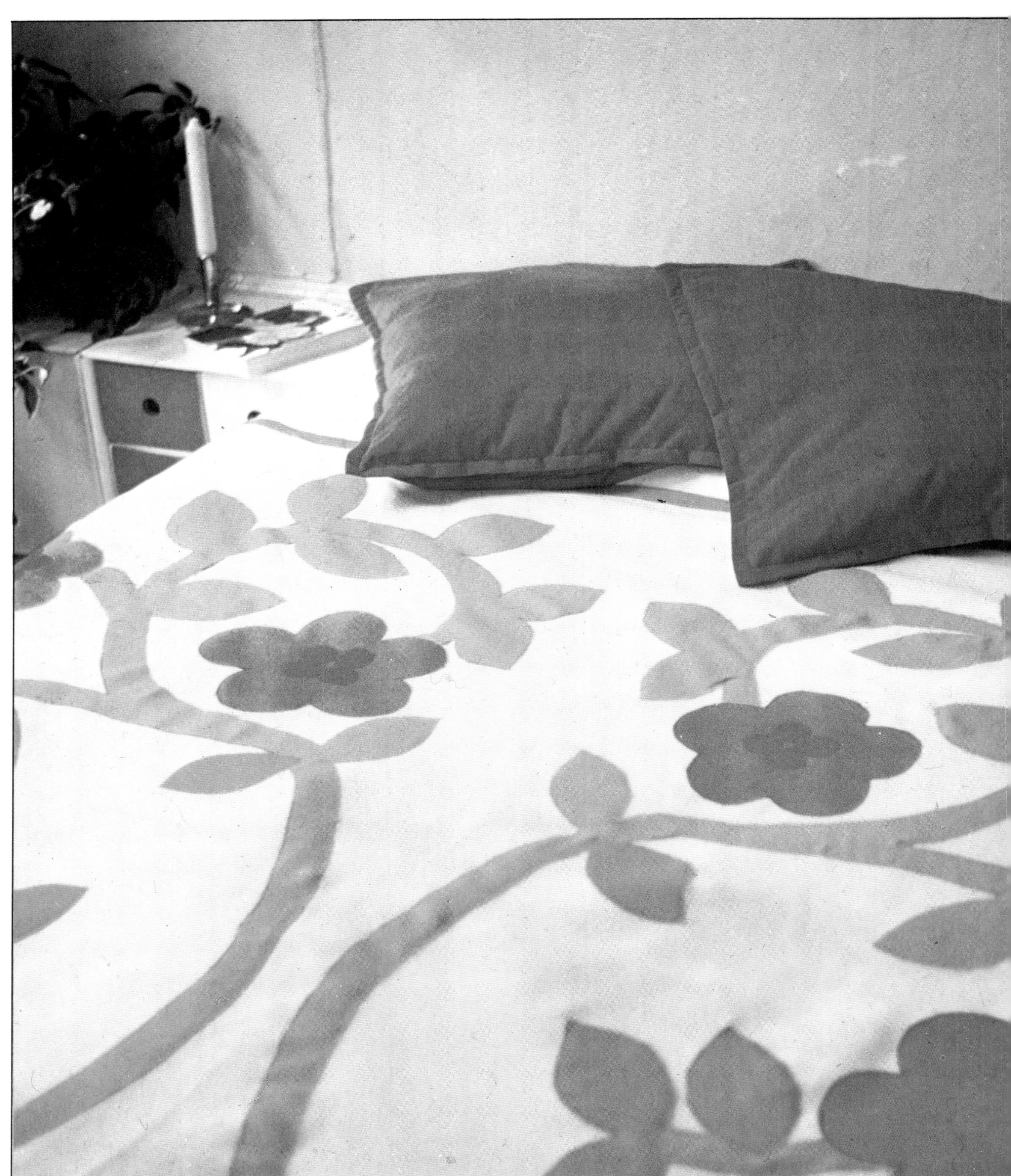

75

This delightful embroidery hanging illustrates the old fairy tale "The Princess and the Pea."

Finished measurement: 13″ deep by 8½″ wide.
Fabric: Canvas, small pieces of fabric remnants, metal foil, absorbent cotton, felt, a white bead, length of yellow thread, and 2 curtain rings.
Embroidery such as this is simple to do, and a young embroiderer might be encouraged to make it for her own bedroom wall. The mattress pieces are stitched to the background on three sides, leaving the top open. Insert a small amount of teased-out absorbent cotton to pad the mattress and close the top with running stitches. Metal foil has been used for the bed frame, the chamber pot and the princess's crown. Cut out the shapes and then prick the stitching holes with a needle.
The foil shapes must be stitched on loosely or they will tear. The pea is a small white bead, stitched finally under the bottom mattress.
After hemming all four sides of the hanging, stitch two curtain rings to the upper corners.
Companion panels can be created from the endless supply of fairy stories, nursery rhymes and poems available in print and folk lore.

76

This charming floral design pillow would look attractive in either a traditional or modern décor

Finished measurement: 15″ × 15″ square.
Fabric: Single weave canvas with 14 threads to 1 inch measuring 21″ by 21″ square. Piece of fabric 16″ by 16″ square for backing. Zipper, 10″ long. Pillow form, 16″ by 16″ square.
Thread: Appleton's Crewel Yarn in amounts indicated in the opposite column.
Needle: Tapestry needle No. 18.
Stitches: Diagonal tent stitch.

Entire design is worked using diagonal tent stitch, worked over two threads of canvas, with three strands of crewel yarn in the needle. When stitchery is complete, block and press as shown on page 122. Trim canvas, leaving ½ inch seam allowances. Make into a pillow, using a fabric backing as shown on page 124, leaving a 10 inch opening on one side, and insert the zipper.

	Color	No.	Skeins
1	Rose pink	759	1
2	Scarlet	505	1
3	Rose pink	755	1
4	Dull rose pink	144	1
5	Dull rose pink	142	3
6	Mauve	607	3
	Mauve	604	1
	Mauve	602	1
	Putty	981	2
	Putty	983	2
	Putty	985	1
	Bright yellow	553	1
	Lemon	996	1
	Chocolate	187	1
	Red brown	208	1
	Honeysuckle yellow	697	1
	Drab green	338	1
	Drab green	335	2
	Drab green	332	2
	Drab green	331	1
	Bright peacock green	835	1
	Bright peacock green	832	1
	Bright peacock green	831	1
	Peacock blue	641	1
	Background—off white	992	12

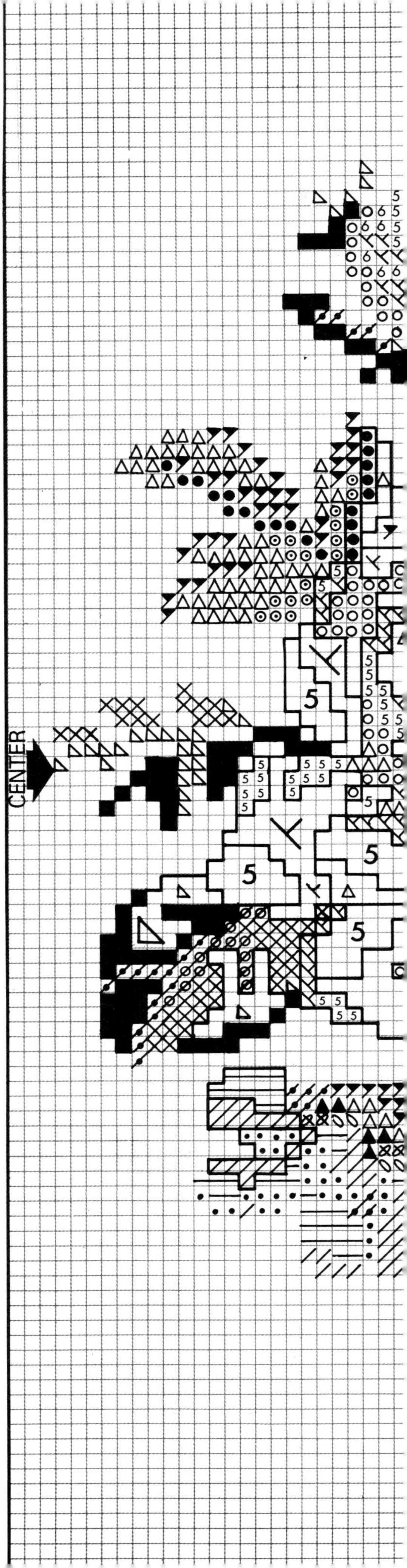

CENTER

CENTER

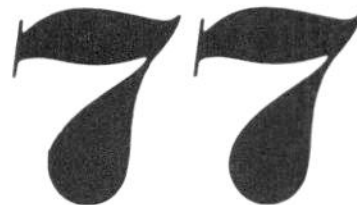

Simplicity is the keynote of this needlepoint panel when applied to a traditionally styled chair and matching pillow.

Finished measurements: $10\frac{1}{2}'' \times 10\frac{1}{2}''$.
Fabric: Double canvas, 10 holes to the inch, 14″ × 14″. Braid, 42 inches plus required length for matching trim for the chair. Matching sewing thread. Embroidery frame.
Threads: D.M.C. Tapestry Yarn, 5 skeins of colors **1** and **2**, two skeins of color **3**, and one each of **4** to **9**:
1. 7469 dark brown; **2.** 7205 clover pink; **3.** 7603 brilliant pink; **4.** 7606 orange; **5.** 7437 yellow/orange; **6.** 7314 blue; **7.** white; **8.** 7548 light green; **9.** 7347 dark green.
Stitches: Cross stitch, herringbone.
Needles: Tapestry needle No. 20. Small curved upholstery needle.

Mark up the centers of the canvas and frame. In cross stitch, a rhythmical working method makes for an evenly finished texture. Follow the chart and work across in rows one below another. Thread needles with each color. Work the given number of stitches and bring the needle up into position ready for that color when it is next used. Continue working with a second color and needle and complete all the colors and background stitches across the row. When the canvas is filled as indicated on the chart, add the straight stitches at the flower centers. Stretch the canvas as shown on page 122. Trim the hem to $1\frac{1}{2}$ inches. Make a single turning leaving canvas the width of the braid. Herringbone stitch the turning to the back of the canvas work, stitch the braid to the panel, and mark the centers of the back of the chair. Match with the panel centers and, working from the centers outward on each side, pin into position. Stitch with the curved needle, taking it down into the panel and up into the chair back. Adjust and smooth as you stitch.

7469
Dark brown

7205
Clover pink

7603
Brilliant pink

7606
Orange

7437
Yellow/orange

7314
Blue

0402
White

7548
Light green

7347
Dark green

78

Stitch a bright Tibetan poppy to add color to a pillow. Or combine a whole garden of poppies in a squared design to form a handsome rug.

Finished measurement: Rug $48\frac{1}{2}$" x $32\frac{1}{2}$". Pillow $8\frac{1}{2}$" x $8\frac{1}{2}$".
Fabric: Canvas about 4 squares to the inch. Rug 52" x 36". Pillow, 11" x 11". Lining 11" x 11".
Threads: Columbia-Minerva Rug yarn. Required number of $1\frac{3}{4}$ ounce skeins in parentheses. First set for the pillow, the second for the rug. **1.** 19 light blue (1) (21); **2.** 21 medium blue (1) (23); **3.** 12 medium gold (1) (5); **4.** 28 avocado (–) (33); **5.** 4 hunter green (2) (37).
Needle: Rug.
Stitches: Cross-stitch.

Mark the horizontal center of the rug. For the first row work from the chart from the center outward to establish the center of the design. From then on, work across the complete row. Omit the avocado from the pillow and continue the border width in hunter green.
Block and make up the rug and the pillow as shown on pages 122, 124.

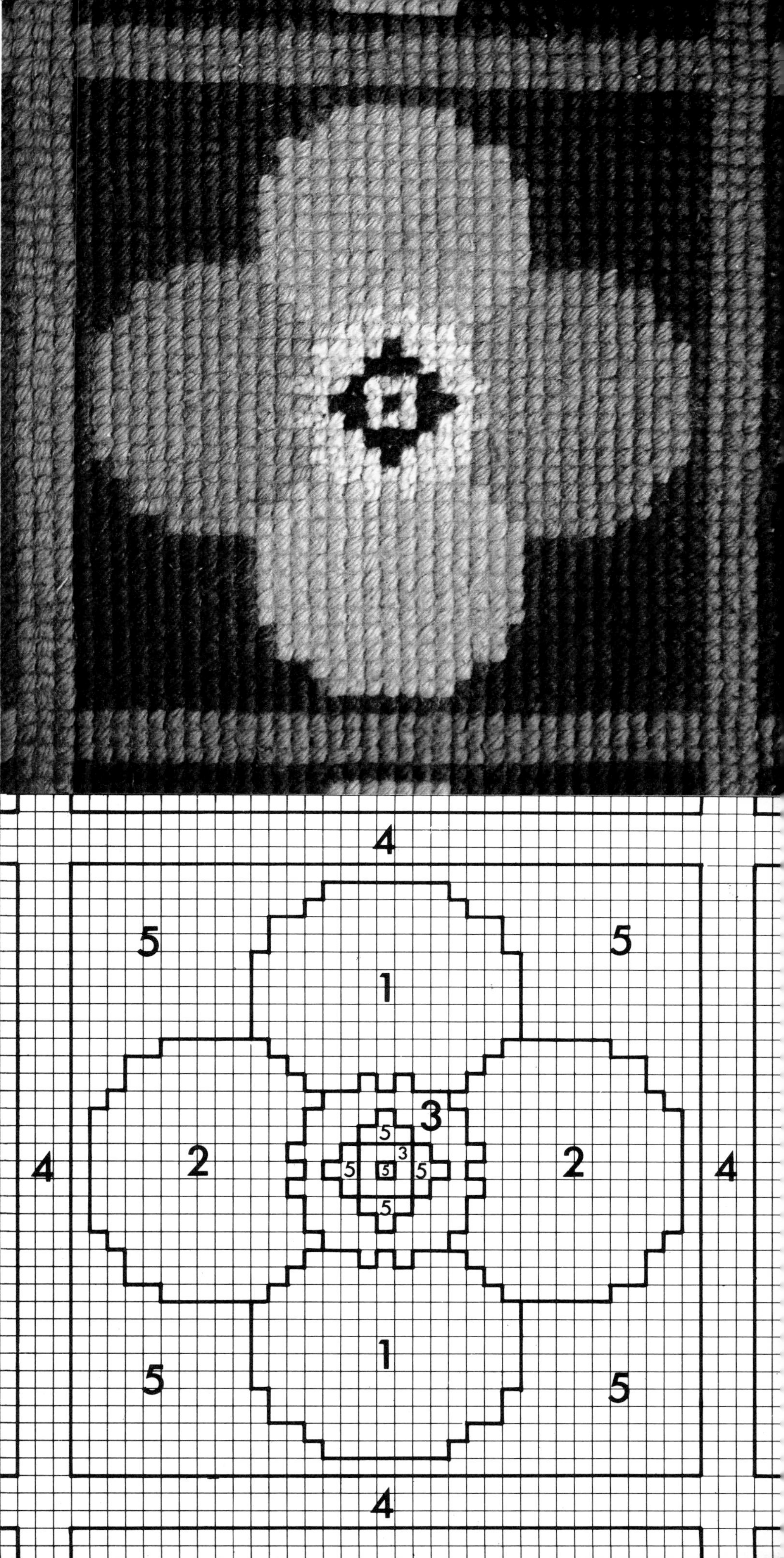

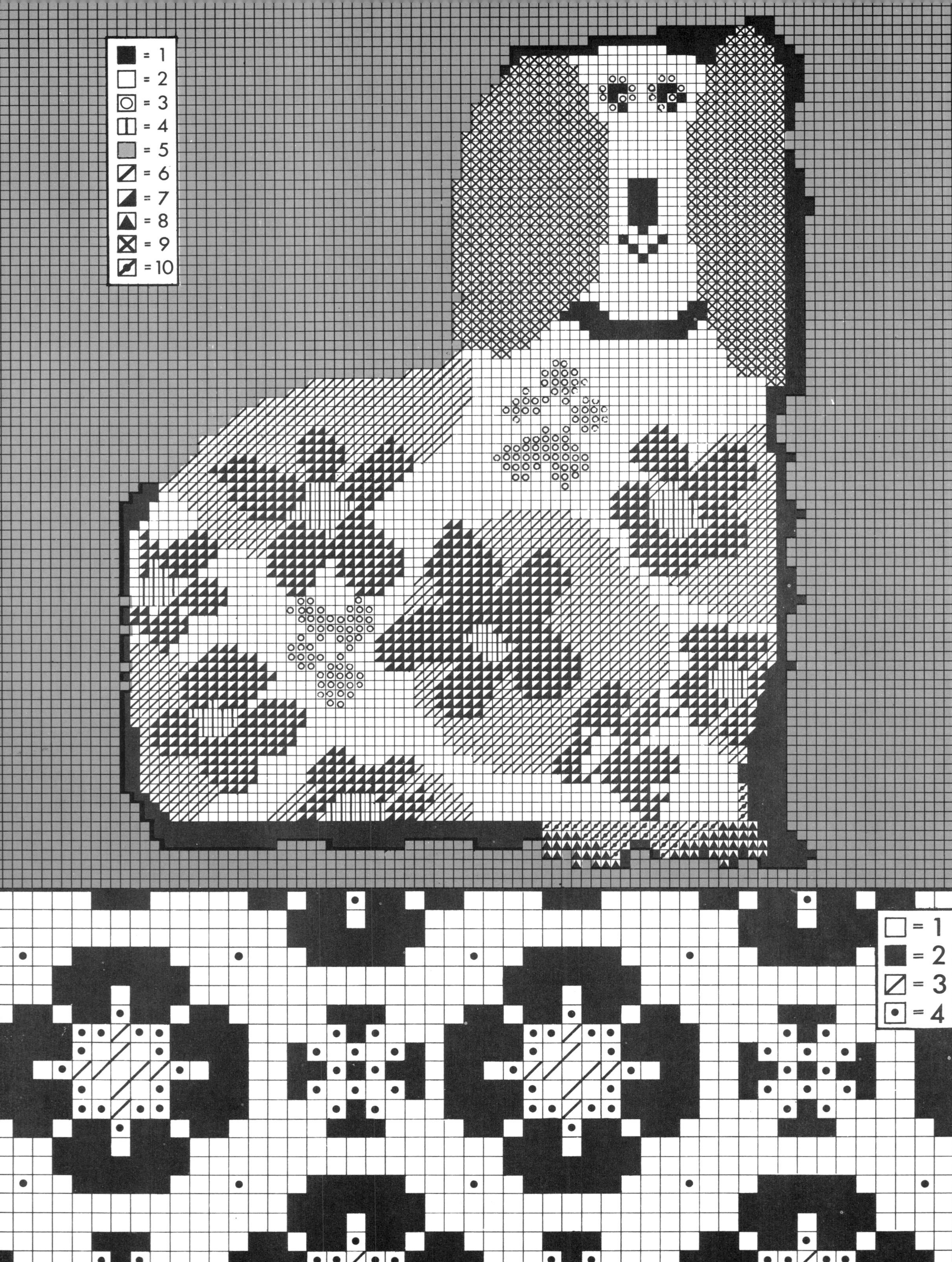
= 1
= 2
= 3
= 4
= 5
= 6
= 7
= 8
= 9
= 10
= 1
= 2
= 3
= 4

79

Daniel the Spaniel lends a splash of color to the nursery or playroom wall.

Finished measurement: About 20″ x 25″.
Fabric: Canvas – 4 stitches to the inch – 24″ x 29″. Lining 22″ x 27″.
Threads: Columbia-Minerva Rug yarn. The number of 1¾ ounce skeins is indicated in parentheses. **1.** 3 black (1); **2.** 1 white (4); **3.** 21 medium blue (2); **4.** 10 yellow (1); **5.** 20 dark aqua (8); **6.** 24 mint (3); **7.** 26 Kelly green (4); **8.** 30 medium brown (1); **9.** 27 forrest green (2); **10.**4 hunter green (1).
Needle: Rug.
Stitch: Cross-stitch.

Mark the center of the canvas. Begin at the top and work the first row from the center outward. From then on, work across each row, changing colors as indicated on the chart. Block and make up as shown on page 122.

80

This lined cross-stitch "carpet" bag with decorative repeat pattern makes an extremely useful holdall.

Finished measurement: About 24″ x 18″.
Fabric: Canvas, 4 stitches to the inch, 22″ x 52″. Lining 22″ x 52″. Yellow fabric for gusset, facing and handles – 1 yard 36″ wide. 48″ long dowel, 4 curtain rings.
Threads: Columbia-Minerva Rug yarn. The number of 1¾ ounce skeins required is in parentheses. **1.** 10 yellow (12); **2.** 28 avocado (15); **3.** 2 off-white (1); **4.** 19 light blue (2).
Needle: Rug.
Stitch: Cross-stitch.

Work each side of the bag separately. Leave sufficient canvas between the worked areas for blocking and making up. Follow the chart and work the repeat pattern as shown in the illustration.
Block and make up as shown for canvas work on page 122. Insert the gusset as shown for the pillow on page 124. At the top of the bag, stitch the facings over the canvas and insert the dowel rods. The handles are made as shown for the handbag, page 123. Blanket stitch over the rings and attach them to the top of the bag. Thread the handle ends through the rings and stitch with strong thread.

Creating your own design/ shape and color

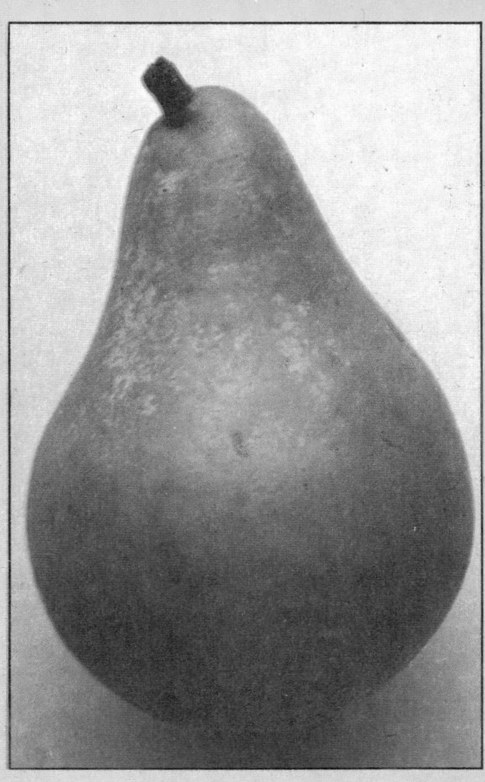

Faced with the idea of creating a design, some embroiderers panic and take refuge in a ready-made embroidery design of some sort. While these are often very good and the result pleasing, all the decisions have been made in advance by someone else, and so the wonderful sense of achievement experienced when one evolves one's own design is lost.

Embroidery is an ideal medium for expressing individuality. With the enormous range of fabrics and threads now available, and a vocabularly of techniques to express the language of design, a whole world of discovery lies at the fingertips of the embroiderer. Once you have mastered a full range of techniques—free embroidery, machine embroidery, black work, canvas work, counted thread, gold work—and you are familiar with the effects which can be achieved, you are ready to start thinking about designs of your own. These and subsequent pages will explain the basic principles of designing, using a simple pear shape throughout for illustration. Drawing inspiration and developing a color sense is covered on these two pages.

All good design represents an individual response to four things: the source of the inspiration, the interpretation, the materials used and the use to which the finished design is put.

Source of inspiration

The world is full of sources of ideas, some of them around your own home. Look at the wood grain on the chopping board in your kitchen for instance, the soap bubbles in the sink as the light dances through them, or the shadows thrown by the leaves of a pot plant. Look at the fruit bowl and the contents of the vegetable rack—fruits and vegetables come in a variety of interesting shapes. Yet, were two people to be inspired by the same shape, the design produced by each of them would be completely different. It is the individual response to inspiration which produces original design.

For the purpose of these and the following pages, a pear shape has been chosen to illustrate the various aspects of design—the texture of stitches, use of color and the ways in which a basic shape can be repeated to produce a complete design for a piece of embroidery. Trace off the pear shape outline and experiment with embroidery techniques.

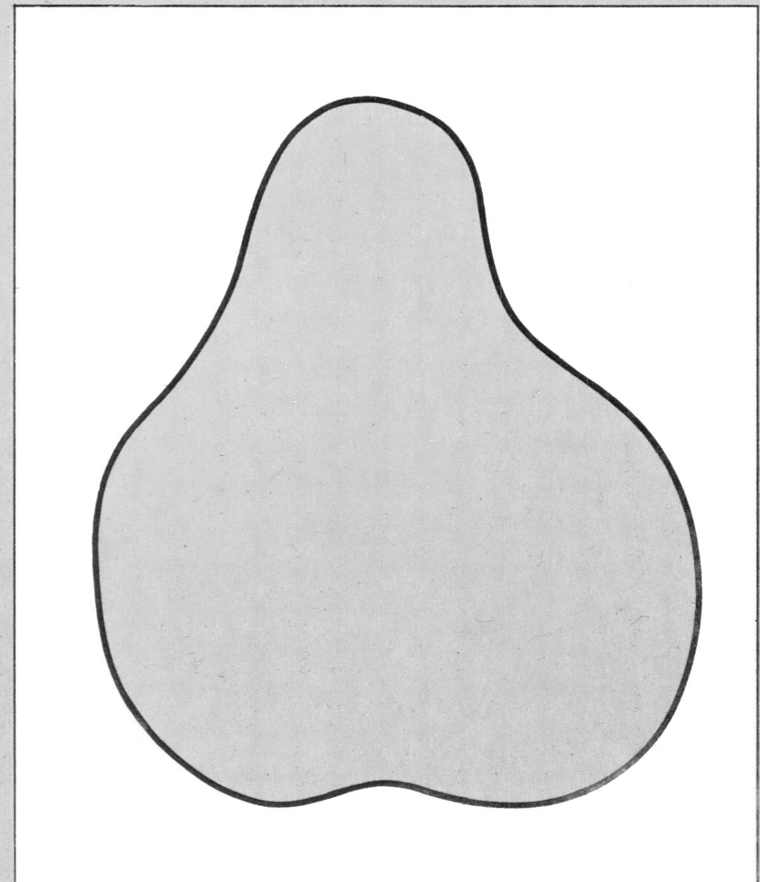

The three embroideries shown here are progressions away from a realistic effect. This pear, worked in tent stitch on canvas, with a satin stitch background, uses closely-related colors in autumn tones to create the roundness and ripeness of the fruit. The focal point of the sample is achieved by the area of highlight in the foreground.

The shapes of things

How does one decide what makes a good shape to begin with. First, it needs to be a simple, open shape to give plenty of scope for experimental stitches. An angular, rigid shape would be boring to work, and a very complicated one would probably take too long to finish. Look at the fruit bowl again and consider the shape of a pear. It is an interesting shape—not too angular, not too regular, it has an adaptable outline and is pleasing to the eye. Many fruit and vegetable shapes would do just as well, but for the purpose of this chapter, the pear shape is used.

Color and tone

In embroidery, the opportunities to experiment with color are endless. The pear shape, embroidered in naturalistic colors, yellow, orange and russet, and in stitches chosen to represent the roundness of the fruit, becomes your interpretation of a plump, ripe, juicy fruit. By choosing combinations of colors, which are not 'pear' colors, a far greater number of designs from the basic shape is possible.

Try experiments with two colors first. Two colors are sufficiently interesting if one color dominates and the other is worked as a small area of true contrast; equal proportions of full strength contrasting colors can appear both harsh and unpleasing. Equal proportions of pale tones, on the other hand, can look monotonous, but if the colors are used in conjunction with stitches, the result can look both subtle and elegant.

It is important to understand that the color of anything is its hue, and the shade of lightness and darkness, its tone. A length of fabric, a patch of grass, or a string of beads may all have the same hue, that is, green, but the tone of each will be different. Several colors can have the same tone and one color, many tones.

A good arrangement of shapes and interesting textures in embroidery can be upset if the tone values are wrong. You can see this if certain areas of the design seem to jump forward too much or if the eye is continually pulled to one corner of the design. At the same time, two or more colors of the same tone can upset the balance, producing a flat, unsatisfying effect. It is rather like eating a meal that begins with cream soup, followed by chicken in white sauce, ending with a mousse. The palate craves the sparkle of melon or the bite of a crisp salad. You can check the tone values of a piece of work by looking at it with the eyes half closed, thus reducing sensitivity to color. The tonal values are immediately emphasized.

Learning color sense

A good color sense can be learned by observing and remembering the combinations of colors in nature; the colors on an autumn leaf, for instance, or on a moss-covered stone, and also by looking at paintings in museums. Notice how color is used in good modern advertising and in magazine and book production. Get into the habit of making brief written notes when you see a color effect that attracts you. Try out schemes for yourself, pinning small swatches of fabric and short end of yarn together, before embarking on a piece of embroidery.

To a certain extent, this pear still achieves a realistic look, and once again uses fairly closely related tones to give the fruit a sunlit look, the highlight being the focal point with tones darkening off towards the edges. This sample is worked in chain stitch and whipped chain stitch and is a comparatively free piece of embroidery.

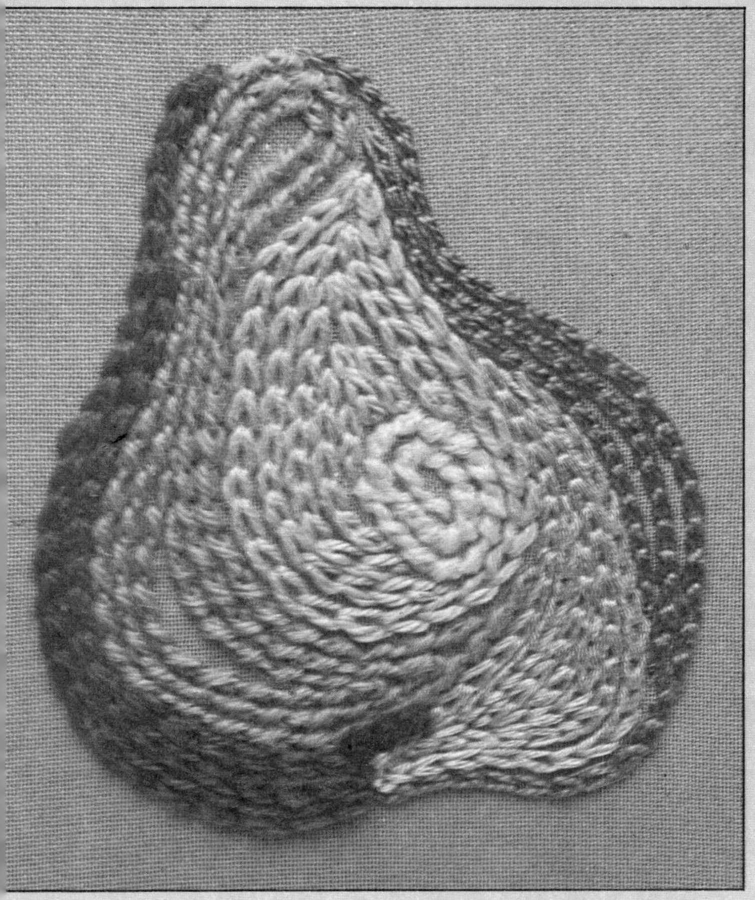

In this interpretation, the designer has opened up the pear to look at the inside, using an appliqué technique, with machine satin stitch and zigzag stitch for contrasting texture. A warm toned tweed is used to indicate the ripeness and texture of the pear's flesh and the bright yellow satin stitch area indicates the shininess of the skin.

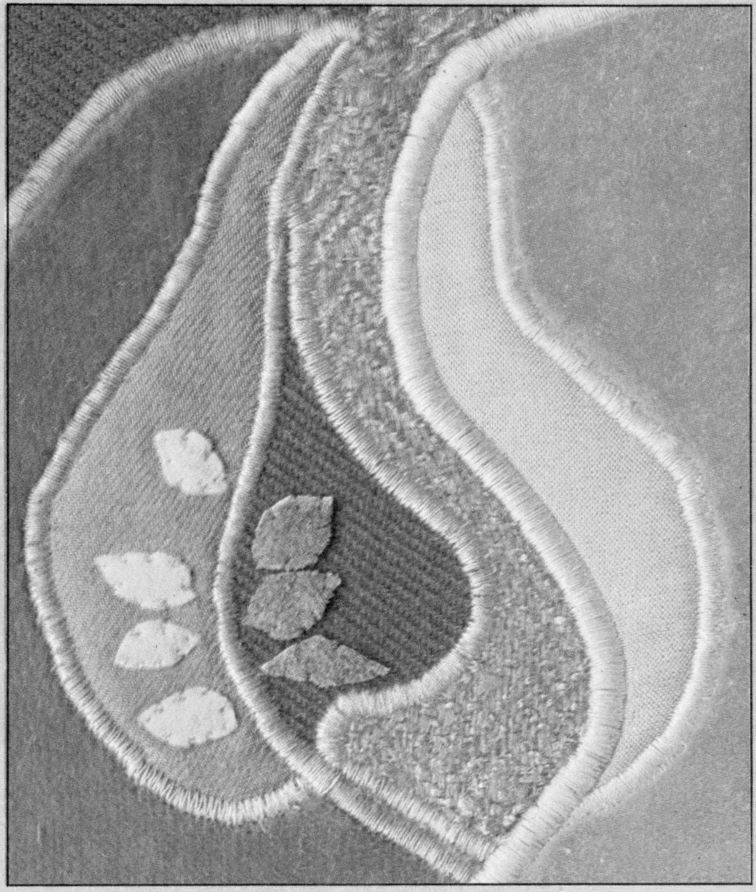

Creating your own design/ texture

In the first chapter, shape, tone and color were considered, and these aspects of design are as important in embroidery as they are in painting. In embroidery, however, the possibilities for creating visually exciting designs through the use of textures is of particular importance. These pages deal with the contrasts, balance and textural effects.

Modern embroidery may at first glance look formless, even chaotic. But it's more like learning a language—once you know the vocabulary, it begins to mean something. The previous two pages showed a good realistic interpretation of a pear; a design that simplified the play of light over the curving surface; and a design that sliced the pear in half, then cut the shape into sections to make a pattern.

Pears 1-3, shown here, are like the "sliced" pear—using the flat shape and cutting it up in different ways to produce a decorative pattern as a vehicle for stitches and color.

Designs 4-6 are freer, more abstract. Lines dissolve, flow, shatter. You might see the mellow ripeness of a pear in 4; or a glistening in sunlight after rain in 5; or 6 may seem quite abstract, like music. So before you start to design, decide whether you want a pattern with stitches and colors, or an impressionistic or abstract picture.

The experienced designer feels subconsciously that a shape is right, that an area needs a denser or more open stitch. The embroiderer new to design consciously has to consider basic principles.

If you plan to make your own design, it's wise to keep the basic shape simple. If your line work is shaky, make a template of the motif; cut it out of paper, cut it up and move the bits around. Or draw around the template, overlapping the outlines until you have a pleasing design. Now plan the stitch areas, having prepared yourself with a repertoire of techniques, a varied collection of fabrics for backgrounds and applied areas, beads, sequins, and buttons.

Texture versus color. It's risky going to town with every stitch and color in the hope that something "modern" will result—it's liable to produce a chaotic effect. If the aim is to exploit texture, do exercise restraint in the range of colors used. If you choose six equally vivid, contrasting colors and six different textures, the vibrations produced by the colors make the texture of secondary importance. Concentrate on ridges and knots, beads, thick and thin threads, slub or nubbly backgrounds, enhanced by closely related colors.

Contrast of texture. Choose stitches that foil each other well, like the curving couched threads with French knots in 4 or the contrast of rough and smooth canvas work textures in 1. With counted thread embroidery, bear in mind the relationship between the background fabric and the embroidery thread. Think of the spaces to be filled as well as the areas to be left unfilled.

Placing the texture. The eye tends to go to the area of maximum contrast of tone and texture, so it is usually better to keep heavier texture away from the edges and corners of a design in a rectangle so that the eye remains close to the central area. Of course, these are only suggestions—if you want a riot of color and texture—go ahead and have fun.

The pears illustrated move even further away from the realistic interpretations on previous pages. The pear is cut in half to show the seeds within the fruit and the texture of the flesh. Yet, at the same time, the feeling of the whole fruit is retained in abstract outline.

The attractive interpretation on the left is worked on canvas using a variety of needlepoint stitches and different textures of thread. The pear below uses a counted thread technique, the background fabric being allowed to contribute to the interesting concept of the design.

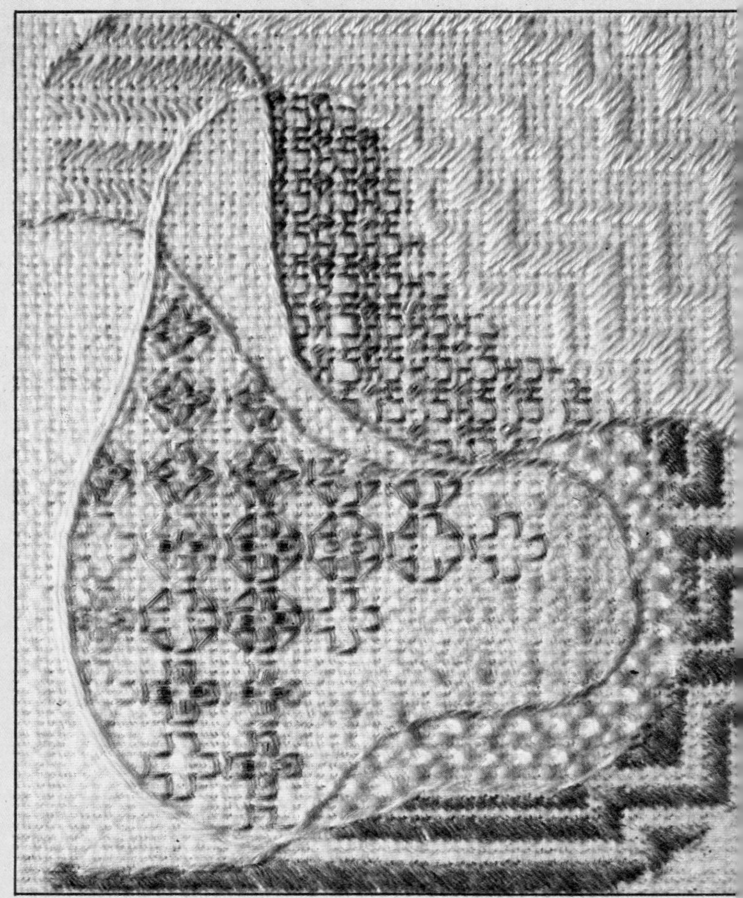

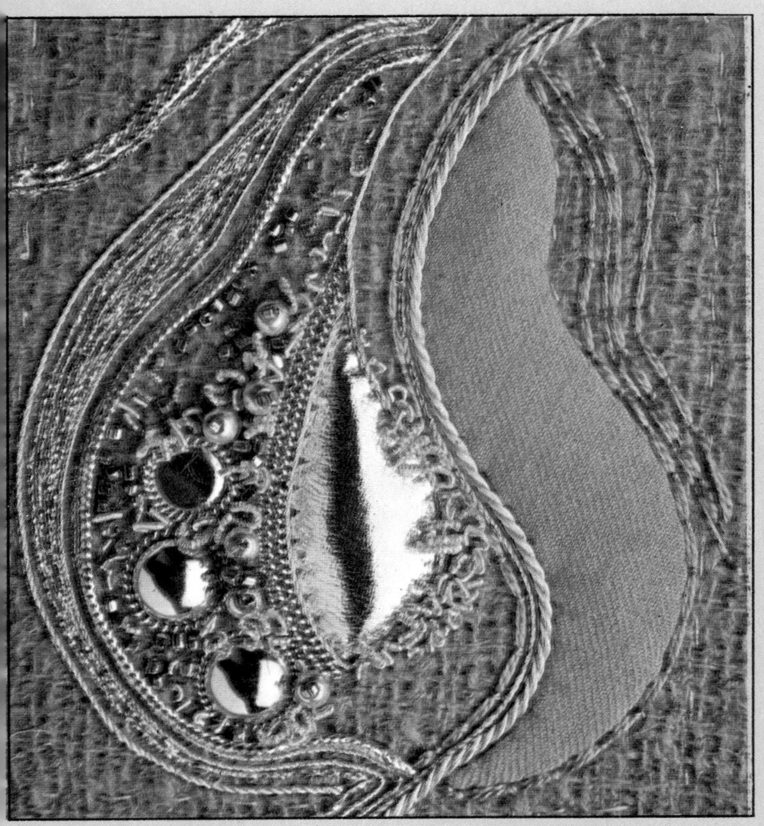

The beautiful metal thread and appliqué pear above is simple in treatment. Color is restricted and the textural contrast is achieved with threads, leather and fabric. The impressionist pear below uses straight stitches, relying on angle and color for the impact of the design.

The pear above is worked in "free texture," which means the use of line and lumpy texture, the embroidery overcoming a strong fabric background. The pear below is almost pure abstract, the seeds enlarged as a concept of the life within and brought outside of the fruit.

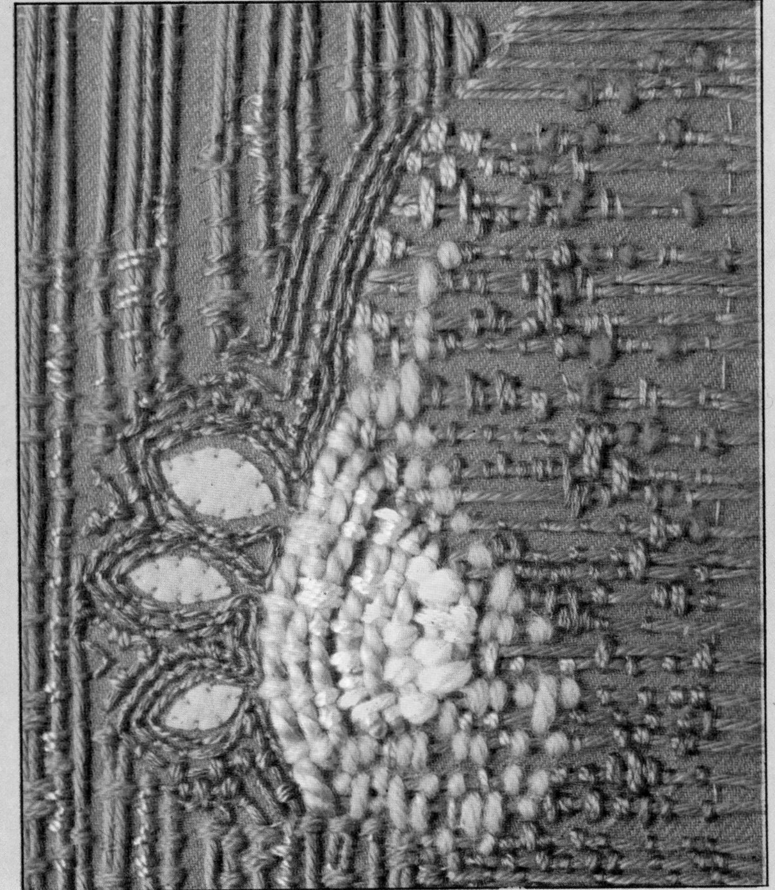

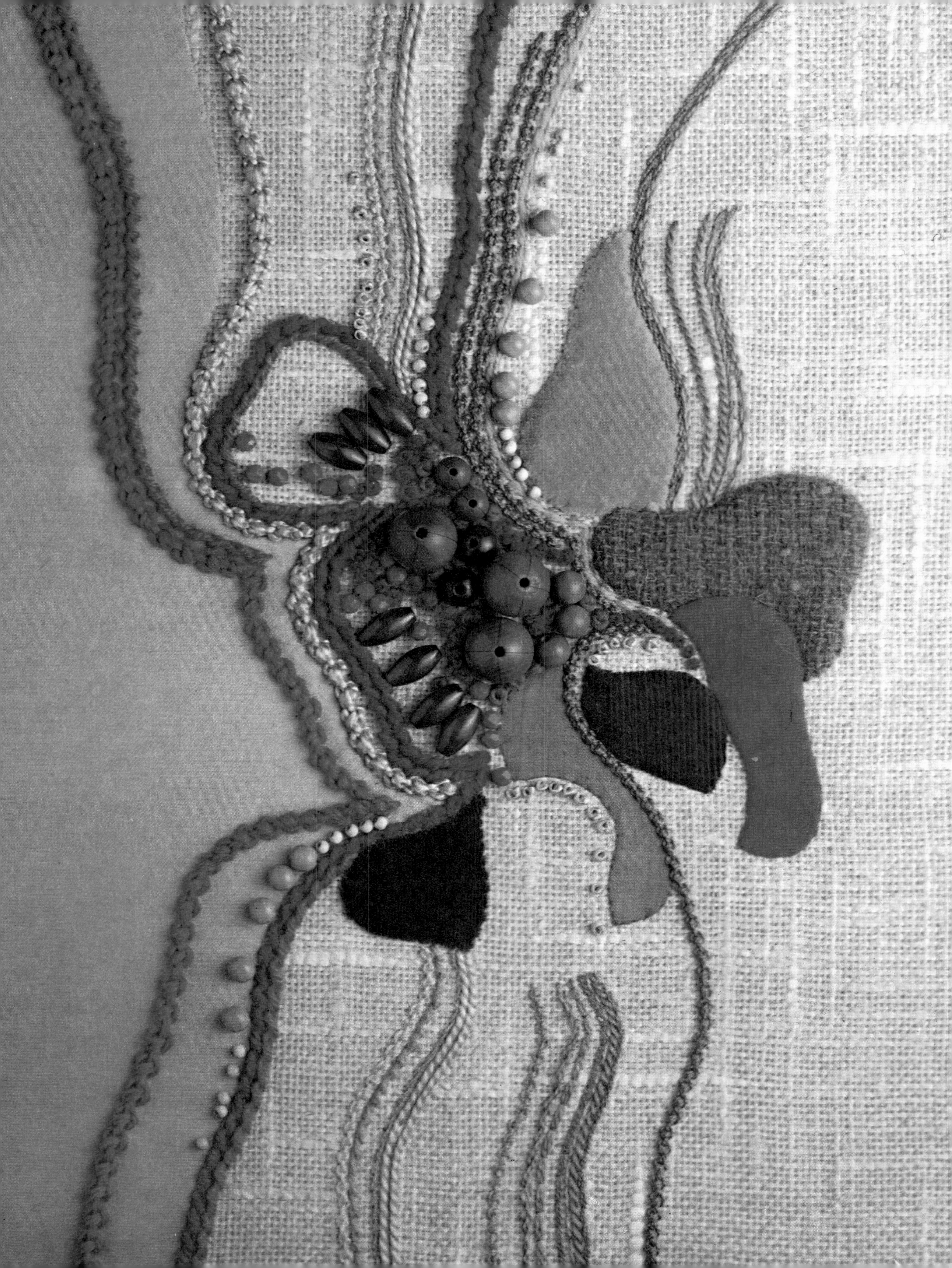

Creating your own design/grouping shapes

Progressing from single shapes, the next stage is to learn how to make a more elaborate design. Still using the original simple pear shape as inspiration, the panel illustrated shows what can be achieved by grouping.

The designer has chosen to create a decorative panel by grouping and overlapping the pear shape, contrasting the texture of heavy slubbed burlap and smooth woolen fabric in the same color and tone for the background. You can try a grouped arrangement like this for yourself by tracing off the pear shape given on page 98 and cutting out several identical pears from several thicknesses of paper. Lay the shapes on a large sheet of paper and move them about until a satisfying arrangement is obtained. In this design the designer has cut away some sections of the pear's outline to give a more subtle effect, and other lines are then added. These lines contrast with the applied areas and link shapes in a free and flowing way, the shapes between being as important to the design as the actual pear shapes. Notice that all the lines and shapes in this design are curved and belong to the same family. The alternative arrangement illustrated shows a quite different approach using parts of the pear shapes which break in and out of rectangles. When this stage is reached, it does not mean that the designing process is complete. The comparative textures and weights of fabric and thread may need reducing or increasing as the work develops. The selection of threads and stitches is part of the design process, inseparable from the overall concept. Things tend to alter all the time unless one is an exceptional visualizer, and it is this that makes designing one's own embroidery so much more exciting and satisfying than copying from someone else's design.

The focal point of the panel illustrated is obtained by grouping different kinds of round shapes, French knots, large wooden beads and woven wheels over beads. Thus the focal point, which is essential to a good design, is achieved—not only because of its placing, but also because it forms the most positive area of texture and color.

The stitches used, mainly twisted chain, double knot stitch, couching and outline are a good choice for lines, because they stand up well from the background. The threads—shiny, highly twisted, soft and matte, vary as much in texture and weight as the fabrics themselves.

Relating embroidery design to use

One should always start by relating an embroidery design to its use, asking oneself whether the object will fit permanently in a room scheme, for instance. Planning the decoration for an embroidered pillow, for example, immediately presents limitations: the general style and color scheme of the room, the shape, fabric and color of the chair or sofa with which the pillow will harmonize or contrast. Is the pillow to form an unobtrusive or a dominant feature? Do the furnishings in the room receive hard wear? What about washing or cleaning? These questions will affect the embroiderer's choice of materials and techniques.

The interests and tastes of the maker and the eventual user of any embroidered object also dictate the choice of design and technique to some extent. Love of animals, flowers, geology, pop art, fishing or brass rubbing—any of these can reveal themselves in design.

The embroiderer who can use a camera will find photography a rich source of ideas. An abstract design might originate from a close-up of bare, gray fig tree branches taken on a Portuguese holiday; a vivid and exciting panel might result from a photograph of the heart of a rose.

Ideas will come at odd moments and should be jotted down as soon as possible—on a theater program, or on the corner of a magazine while on a journey. Ideally, the student of design should always carry a small sketch book with her, which easily can become a reference source for many creative hours.

Summarizing the principles of embroidery design discussed in these pages, two different designs were worked out by an embroiderer using the pear shape as a basic motif (see diagrams below). She traced off and cut out several pear shapes and then arranged and rearranged them under a sheet of tracing paper until a pleasing design appeared. She then drew the outlines of the paper shapes using a soft pencil, and rubbed out some parts of the outlines and added other lines and solid areas, roughing in those which were eventually to become textured and contrast areas.

The piece of embroidery illustrated shows how the embroiderer finally interpreted one of her original inspirations (the diagram on the left) into threads, fabric and beads. Two textured fabrics have been used for the background, a thick, coarsely woven burlap and a smooth, even-weave fabric. The pear shapes themselves have been treated in a variety of ways; some are cut from fabric—velvet, wool jersey, tweed, silk—and applied to the background, others are incorporated into the design in embroidery threads and stitches or outlined in silk cord. The embroidery stitches chosen by the designer are mainly twisted chain, outline stitch, double knot stitch and couching. Beads were used for the focal part of the embroidery, some grouped in the center and others used in graduated sizes. Tones of purple, chosen for the strongest colors in the design, are repeated in the beads, large wooden ones for the central area, with smaller ones grouped around.

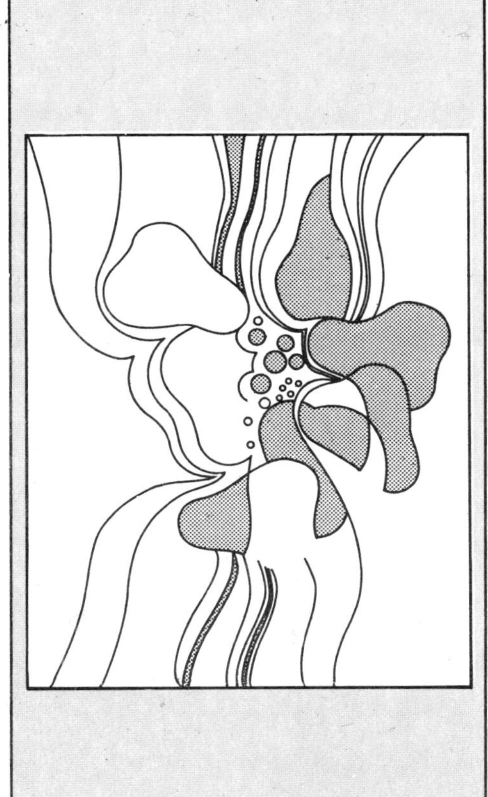

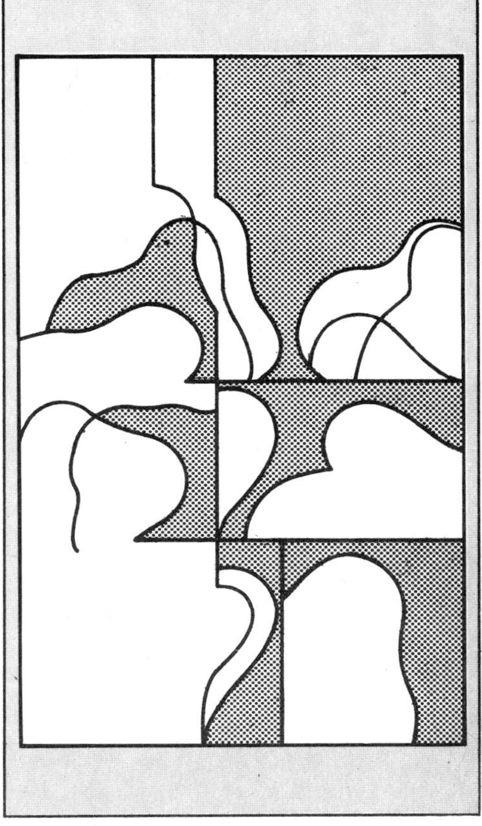

This fabric collage and embroidery picture, entitled "Fossil," was designed by Marjorie Self and measures about 2 feet square. Openweave linen fabrics are used for the background, and the velvet shapes which spring from the focal point are fabric-covered polystyrene pieces, glued to the background. Surface embroidery, in rug wool, and knitting wool, is worked in raised chain band and stem stitch, and the fascinating web effect is achieved with freely worked strands of linen thread, interwoven with tapestry wool in Cretan stitch.

Instructions to complete the previous pages

Hedgerow

Finished measurement: 14″ square for both pillow and picture (excluding frame).
Pillow
Fabric: White linen 12″ × 12″. Sage green satin or any close-weave material, 15″ × 15″. Pillow form, 16″ × 16″.
Thread: Sewing thread, sage green.
Picture
Fabric: White linen 15″ × 15″. Sage green fabric 15½″ × 15″.
Mat board, 2 pieces, 14″ × 14″.
Fabric adhesive. Picture frame.
Pillow and picture
Threads: 1 skein D.M.C. 6-strand floss in each of the following colors: **1.** 972 gorse yellow; **2.** 335 rose pink; **3.** 608 orange; **4.** 783 muscat green; **5.** 3052 moss green; **6.** 895 dark moss green; **7.** 3346 grass green; **8.** 729 azure; **9.** 995 perriwinkle.
Needles: Crewel needles Nos. 6 and 7. Sharp needles to use for plain sewing.
The embroidery method is the same for both the pillow and the picture. Use four strands of thread for color No. 1—gorse yellow; one strand for color No. 4—muscat green; and two strands for the remaining color.
Mark the center of the fabric in each direction and transfer the design to the fabric, using the method shown on page 121. Frame the fabric as shown on page 122.
The stitchery is freely worked and for success in this apparently casual embroidery, stitch with the growing points of the leaves and flowers in mind, shaping the lines and curves as you stitch. The type and direction is indicated on the outline diagram.
Work the underlying areas, such as the petals and large flowers, first. Make up as shown on page 125.

65 Blackwork tablecloth

Finished Measurement: Approx. 57″ × 57″.
Fabric: $1\frac{5}{8}$ yards 59 inch wide, pale-blue, even weave embroidery linen.
Thread: D.M.C. Pearl Cotton No. 8, 5 balls black 0403.
Needle: Tapestry needle No. 24.

Square the fabric and mark the center each way with lines of basting stitches. The photograph below gives one quarter of the design. The center is the upper left-hand corner of the photograph and this should coincide with the basting stitches on the fabric. The number within the bracket indicates the number of threads between the center section of the design and the border. Note also the arrangement of the stitches on the threads of the fabric. Commence the embroidery at the top of each central flower motif, 36 threads down from the crossed basting stitches, and work the center section and border section as given. Repeat in reverse from the left-hand edge of the photograph to complete one half of the design. Then turn the fabric and work the other half in the same way.

Press as shown on page 122. To finish, turn back a one inch hem on all the edges, miter the corners and slip stitch as shown on page 123.

center

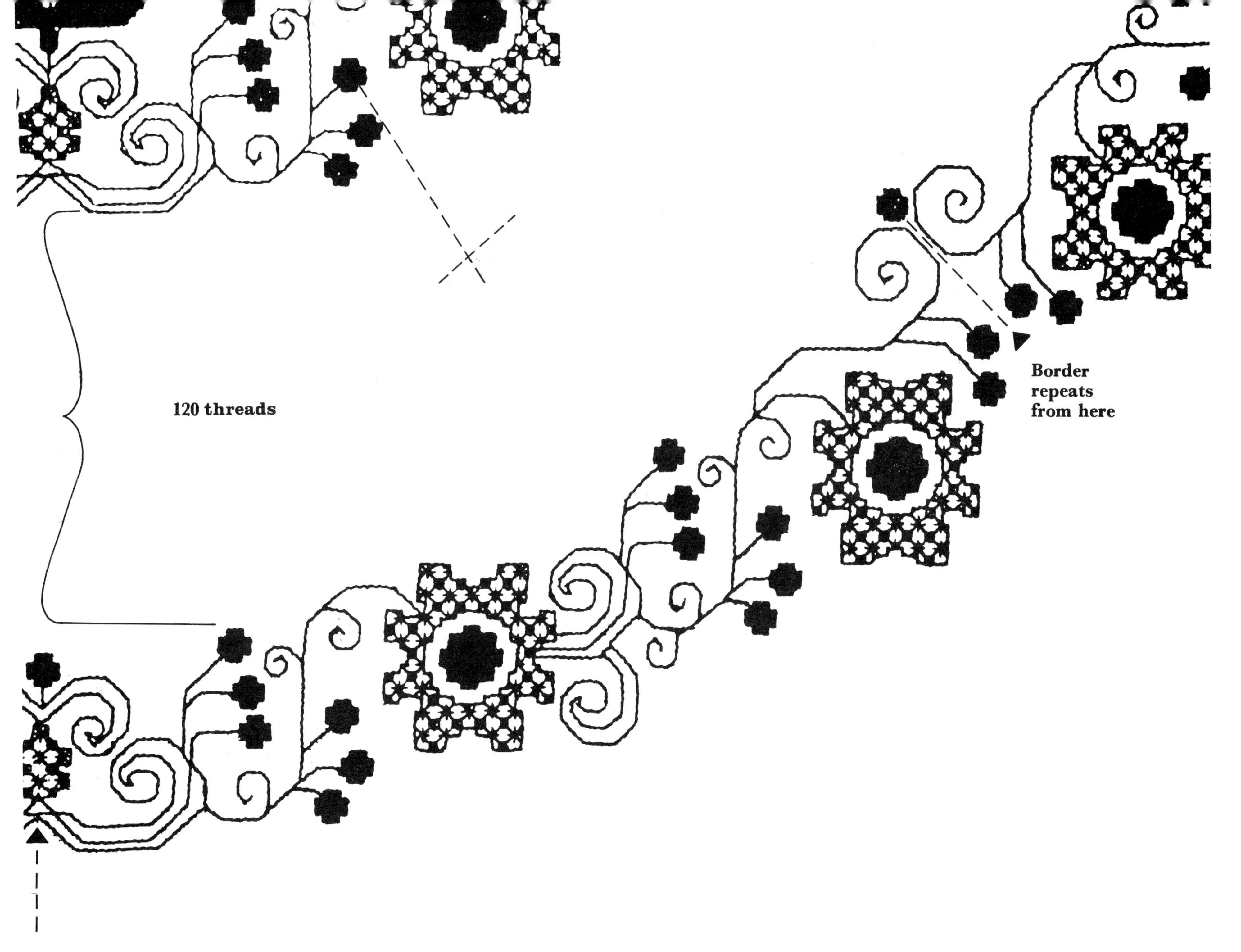
120 threads
Border
repeats
from here

66 *Table runner*

Finished Measurement: 50″ long x 14″ wide.
Fabric: ½ yard 59 inch wide, even-weave linen with 21 threads to 1 inch, blue.
Threads: D.M.C. Pearl Cotton No. 8, 3 balls. Sewing thread to match linen.
Needle: Crewel needle No. 16.
Stitches: Cross-stitch, Holbein or double running stitch.
With basting stitches mark the center of the fabric vertically and horizontally following the grain of the fabric. Work the design from the chart over two threads of fabric each way. The main part of the design is worked in cross-stitch and the fine lines in Holbein or double running stitch. Work twenty-one complete repeats of the design down the center along the length of the cloth. Finish the edges of the runner with a 1 inch deep hem, mitering the corners neatly as shown on page 123.

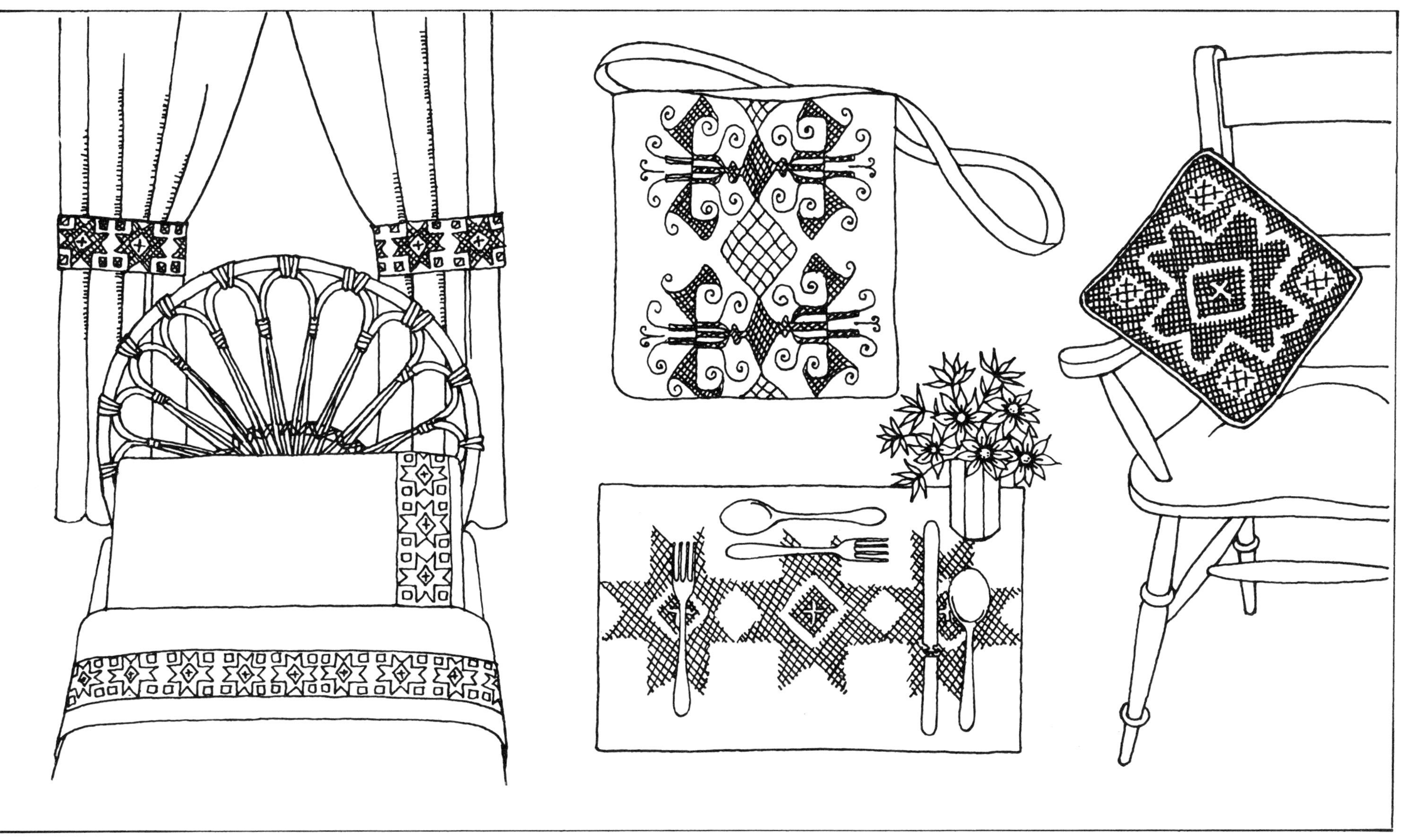

Here are four suggestions of ways in which the design can be applied to fashion and home accessories.

67 - 71

Five floral pillows

Rhododendron pillow

Threads: D.M.C. 6-strand floss in: **1.** Gray blue 806; **2.** Medium blue 826; **3.** Light blue 813; **4.** Light green 955; **5.** Dark green 905; **6.** Dark blue 939. Two skeins each of numbers 1-5. One skein of number 6.
Stitches: Long and short stitch, French knots.
Using two strands in the needle, work flowers and leaves in long and short stitch. Begin by working the underlying leaves and petals. The upper petals should be stitched slightly into those below to make a clear-cut line. Slant the stitches toward the center of the flowers and the central vein of the leaf. French knots should be worked into the finished embroidery.

Thistle pillow

Threads: D.M.C. 6-strand floss in: **2.** Dark turquoise 517; **3.** Light turquoise 807; **4.** Gray/blue 806; **5.** Olive green 987; **6.** Yellow/green 988; **7.** Dark green 986. Color number 1. Navy blue crewel wool. Three skeins each of colors 1 and 2, and two skeins each of the remaining colors.
Stitches: Satin, French knots, long and short and outline stitch.
For the flower centers, use two strands of crewel wool in the needle. Some of the centers are worked in satin stitch and others filled with French knots. The rest of the embroidery is worked with three strands of floss in the needle. The flowers are worked in satin stitch, the leaves in long and short stitch and the stems in outline stitch.

Anemone pillow

Threads: D.M.C. 6-strand floss in: **1.** Dark blue 336; **2.** Medium blue 312; **3.** Light blue 334; **4.** Yellow green 701; **5.** Dirty green 890; **6.** Green 986. One skein of color 1, two skeins each of colors 4, 5 and 6, and three skeins each of colors 2 and 3.
Stitches: Long and short stitch.
Using three strands of floss in the needle, work the design in long and short stitch. Start on the large flower, using light blue color 3, then embroider with medium blue color 2. Finally, work the center of the flower and the streaks in dark blue color 1. Work the buds in the same order, stitching the dark blue streaks last.

Peony pillow

Threads: Two skeins of D.M.C. 6-strand floss in: **1.** Light blue 813; **2.** Medium blue 826: **3.** Light blue/lilac 334; **4.** Dark blue/lilac 336; **5.** Light lilac 209; **6.** Dark blue 939; **7.** Bright green 911; **8.** Dark green 890; **9.** Olive green 469.
This design is worked entirely in long and short stitch, using two strands of thread in the needle. Commence working the design from the center of the flower with the stitches lying in the direction indicated on the tracing pattern.

Gypsophila pillow

Threads: D.M.C. 6-strand floss in: **1.** Light violet 334; **2.** Dark violet 312; **3.** Blue 826; **4.** Turquoise 519; **5.** Light green 955; **6.** Yellow/green 472; **7.** Dark green 905.
Two skeins each of colors 4, 6 and 7. Three skeins each of colors 1, 2, 3 and 5.
Using two strands of thread in the needle, the flowers and leaves are worked with long and short stitch. Stitch the petals and the flowers first; then fill in the centers with satin stitches and French knots. Allow the satin stitches at the centers to radiate a little into the petals. With three strands of thread in the needle, work all stems in outline stitch.

When all the embroidery is completed, press the work carefully on the wrong side. Make into a pillow measuring 15″ square as shown on page 124 and then insert a zipper centrally along one seam on the pillow. Press and insert pillow form.

Rhododendron pillow

Thistle pillow

Anemone pillow

Peony pillow

Gypsophila pillow

72 *Framed peony*

Finished measurement: 11″ x $10\frac{1}{2}$″.
Fabric: White linen $12\frac{1}{2}$″ x 12″.
Threads: D.M.C. 6-strand floss, one skein of each. **1.** 776 light carnation (4 strands); **2.** 3326 mid carnation (4 strands); **5.** 608 mid flame (4 strands); **6.** 718 mid cyclamen (4 strands); **7.** 915 deep cyclamen (4 strands); **9.** 369 light almond green (3 strands); **10.** 320 mid almond green (3 strands); **12.** 906 parrot green, 904 moss green (mix 2 strands of each). Bucilla Crewel Wool. 1 card of each, 2 strands in the needle. **3.** 9 light rose; **4.** 35 medium red; **8.** 86 fuchsia; **11.** 29 dark olive.
Needles: Crewel needle No. 6. (stranded floss); Chenille No. 22. (crewel wool).
Stitches: Satin, chain, stem.

Mark the fabric with the design as shown on page 121. Work the embroidery as indicated in the outline diagram. Begin with the petals which appear to lie underneath. The stitching of the upper petals encroaches slightly on the under. Prepare for framing as shown on page 122.

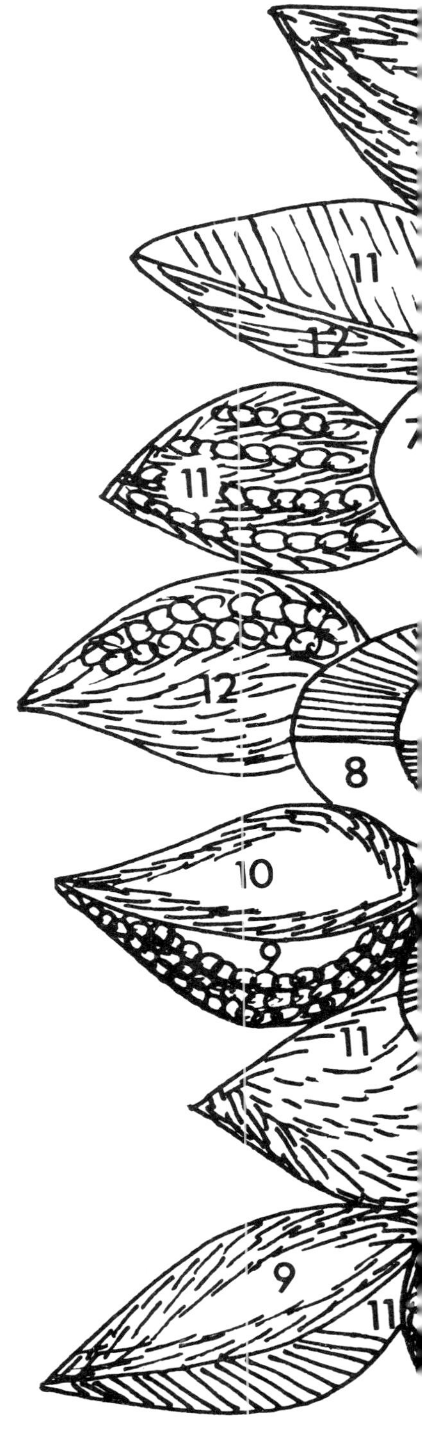

73 *Summer handbag*

Finished measurement: Approx. 10″ × $10\frac{1}{2}$″.
Fabric: White even weave linen, 2 pieces 12″ × 12″.
Lining, 2 pieces, 12″ × 12″.
Non-woven interfacing fabric, 2 pieces, 12″ × 12″.
White sewing thread.
Handbag frame, 10″ wide.
Threads: D.M.C. 6-strand floss, 3 skeins of **1**, eight skeins of **4**, and one each of the remainder.
1. 350 geranium; **4.** 742 gorse yellow; **7.** 301 chestnut; **8.** 445 canary yellow; **9.** 310 black. Appleton's Crewel Yarn, two skeins, of **2** and **6** and one of **3** and **5. 2.** 804 fuchsia; **3.** 566 sky blue; **5.** 405 sea green; **6.** 545 early English green
Crewel needle No. 5
Sharps needle
Stitches: Satin, buttonhole, French knots, brick.
Mark the center of the pieces of linen fabric and transfer the design to the fabric as shown on page 121. The shading on the trace design indicates the type and direction of the stitches. For the most satisfactory results work the looped buttonhole stitches without a frame and the flat, satin stiches in a frame. With six strands of thread work the small flowers, (geranium, color **1**) with straight stitches and finish at the center with a French knot. Six strands of thread are used for the two brick stitch flowers (gorse yellow, color **4**). Use two strands of crewel yarn and three strands of floss for other parts of the design. Press the finished embroidery and then interline as shown on page 122.

Join the back and front of the bag. Make a hem at the top edges to fit the rods. Cut, make up and fit the lining. Slip stitch in position.

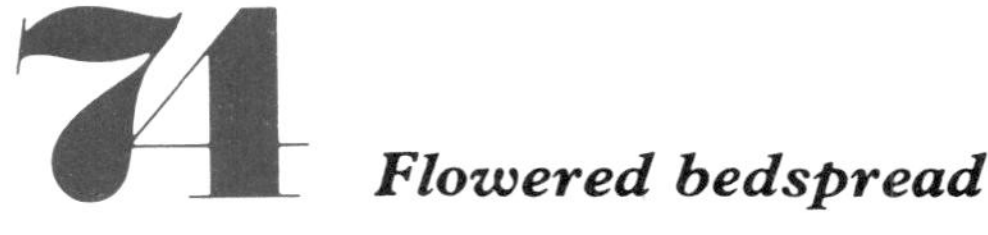

74 *Flowered bedspread*

Finished measurement: 100″ × 70″.
Fabric: 4½ yards 54 inch wide heavy woolen fabric, or a ready-made bedspread. Pieces of lightweight woolen fabric in following colors and amounts: ½ yard dark pink, ⅝ yard pink, 1½ yards green, 2 yards dark green.
Thread: Sewing.
Needle: Crewel needle No.8.

Cut the 4½ yard length of fabric in half making two 2¼ yard lengths. Cut one of these lengths in half along the crease line of the fabric. With a flat fell seam join a narrow panel to either side of the wide panel. Press well.
Spread the bedspread flat. Make a template and cut out flowers and leaves from the colored fabrics. Arrange them on the bedspread and pin them down. Baste in place and link the flowers and leaves with curving stems cut from scraps of fabric. Alternatively, stems could be embroidered.
Using a zigzag stitch on a machine, stitch around the shapes. If preferred, the shapes can be cut with narrow turnings, the raw edges turned and basted to the wrong side. Then apply to the background with a slip stitch or fine hemming stitches. Finish the edges with a 1 inch deep bias cut border in the dark green fabric.
Alternative techniques: The simple flower and leaf shapes also could be worked in machine embroidery for a different effect. Crewel wool embroidery would be effective, too, using long and short stitches and French knots. For a combination of appliqué and surface embroidery techniques, work the flowers in chain stitch, working large stitches around and around to the center of the petals. The stems could be made of flat braid applied to the surface.

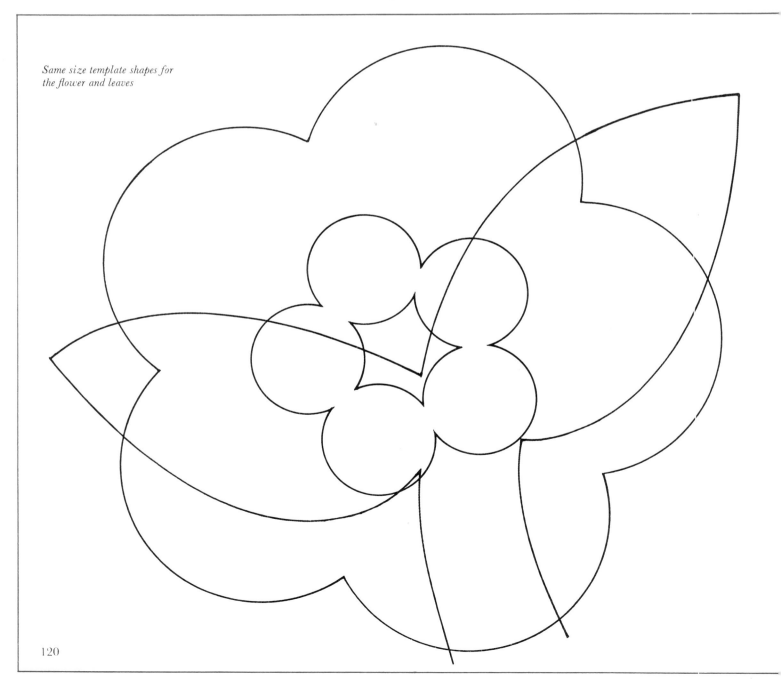

Same size template shapes for the flower and leaves

Technical know-how

Enlarging a design

With a ruler and pencil, enclose the outline drawing in a square or rectangle. Draw center lines horizontally and vertically and divide these again. Draw a separate rectangle to the size required and divide in the same manner. Copy the outlines from the smaller to the larger squares. Letters and figures help to identify the squares.

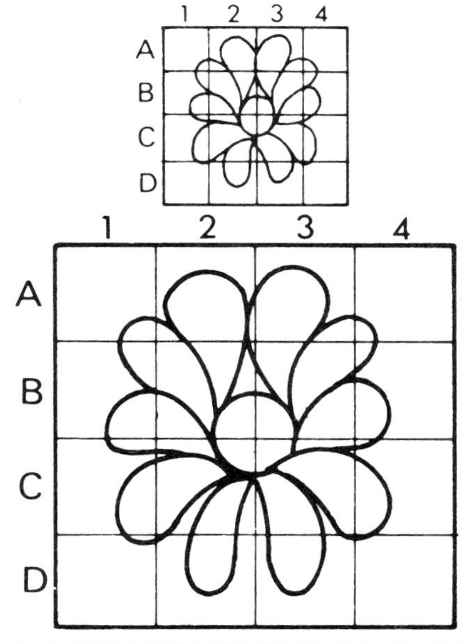

To prepare the fabric

Overcast the edges of the fabric to prevent fraying during working.

Template

Simple shapes cut in thin cardboard are useful for repeating patterns. Trace the shape required onto the card, cut around it, pin in position on fabric and draw around it with pencil. Or, mark with pins, remove the cardboard and baste around the pinned outline. Where fabric has to be applied, use the same cardboard to cut the shape, adding a seam allowance if fabric has to be stitched by hand.

To work from a chart

With running stitch, mark the centers of the linen or canvas. Each square on the chart represents a stitch. Follow the pattern on the chart and work each stitch onto the canvas. When working in cross-stitch, begin at one end and work the design and background in rows. To begin, work a few stitches, leaving a length of thread on the surface. Thread into the back of the worked stitches, and fasten off in the same way. Or, where possible, bring the thread to the front of the canvas and leave. The next stitches will cover the loose thread left at the back, and the thread at the front is cut off.

To trace the drawn outline

Baste horizontal and vertical center lines onto the fabric. Trace the given outline onto tissue paper, mark the centers, and pin the tracing into position on the fabric. Use the basted lines as a guide. With running stitch and one strand of thread, outline the design. Use the color of the finished embroidery. A smaller stitch on the surface than underneath allows for the easy removal of the tissue paper. Remove the pins and tear the paper away carefully. Round-ended tweezers are useful for pulling off any fragments of tissue paper caught in the stitches. The guide lines and colors are laid out clearly on the fabric and they become part of the embroidery and need not be removed when the work is finished. For organdy: draw the traced line onto the tissue paper with a pen. Pin to the BACK of the organdy. The design can be seen through the fabric and outlined with running stitch. There is no need to pierce the paper.

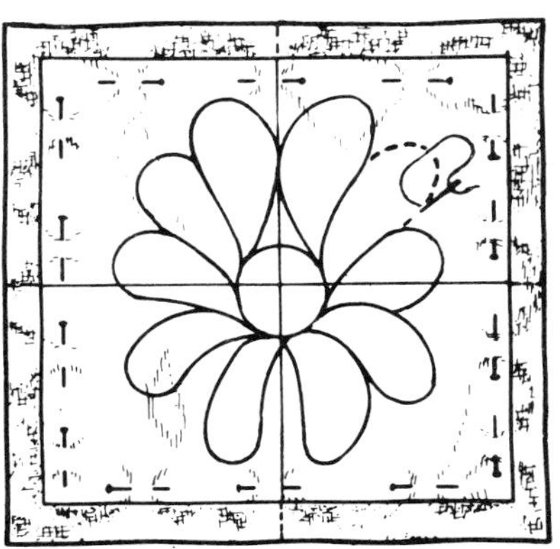

Embroidery frames

A frame is helpful for the even working of some techniques. There are two basic types, the hoop and the frame.

The hoop. It consists of an inner and an outer hoop. The outer has an adjustable screw, and the fabric is gripped taut between the two hoops. Easily positioned and removed it is useful for working on a large area and is also useful when an embroidery has a variety of stitches, some of which may be worked more easily in and some out of the hoop.
Hoops with a screw clamp for fixing to the table, or with a stand, are the most useful as they leave both hands free for working.
To mount the fabric: Separate the inner and outer hoops, and place the fabric over the inner hoop. A square of tissue paper will prevent hoops marking the fabric. Push outer hoop into position, and tear away center of the tissue paper and tighten hoop screw. To avoid stretching the fabric, be sure that the weave lies vertical and horizontal.

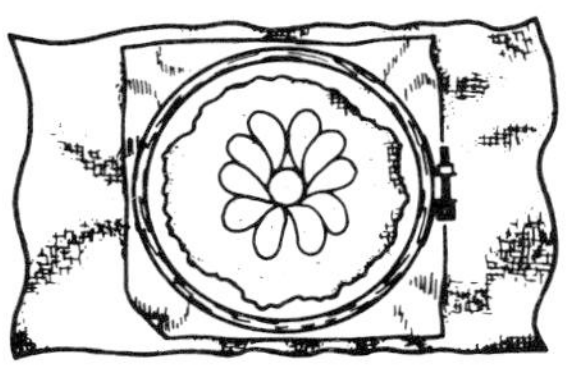

The frame. This holds the whole area of the fabric firmly and is obtainable in several sizes from 18″ wide.
When the fabric is mounted, support the frame between two tables or a table and chair. Both hands should be free to work, one above and one below the fabric. The diagram shows how to mount the fabric. Mark the centers of the webbing at each end of the frame, make a single hem at each end of the fabric to be mounted and mark the center. Place the centers together and overcast fabric to frame. Begin at the center and work outward, and repeat at the opposite end. Insert the side slats and fix in position with cotter

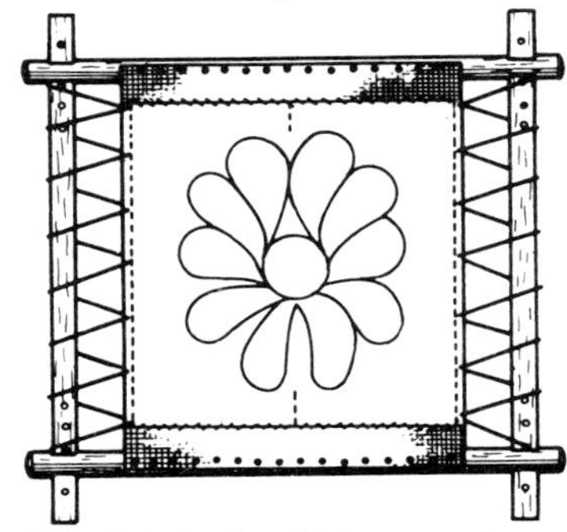

pins. The fabric should be taut, but not strained. Baste a hem along the sides, laying in a piece of string to strengthen it. Begin at the center and, with a packing needle and fine string, lace the side of the fabric to the side supports. Tighten evenly at each side and knot the string firmly.

Pressing and blocking

To press embroidery – pad a large, flat surface with a blanket and ironing cloth. Lay the embroidery face downward and press with a damp cloth.
To block needlepoint – pad a board with clean, damp blotting paper. Place the needlepoint face upward on the blotting paper, and starting at the center, fix one end of the canvas with thumbtacks. Align the horizontal threads with the edge of the board. Repeat at the opposite end and at the sides. Leave to dry for at least twenty four hours.

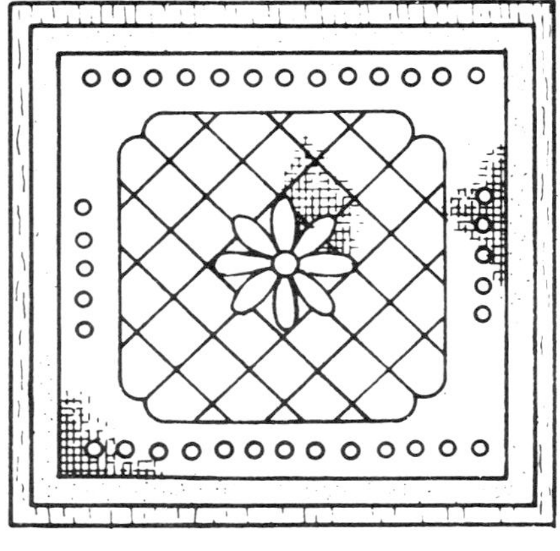

To prepare embroidery for a picture frame

Cut a piece of cardboard or hardboard to fit frame, mark centers and match with embroidery. Turn edges of fabric over the cardboard and stitch firmly in place with strong thread. Start from the center and work outward. Tighten thread so that there is an even pull on the fabric and fasten off securely. Repeat for the two remaining sides. When choosing frame allow sufficient depth to prevent embroidery from pressing on the glass. Embroidery shows to best advantage without glass in the frame.

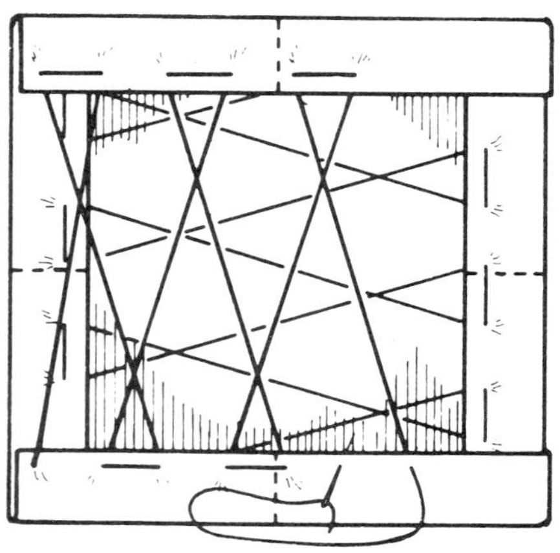

Making up with an interlining

(Belt, glasses case, shopping bag and handbag etc.) The basic method is the same for each.
Cut interlining to fit within the hem lines. Lay the decorated fabric face downward and pin the interlining in

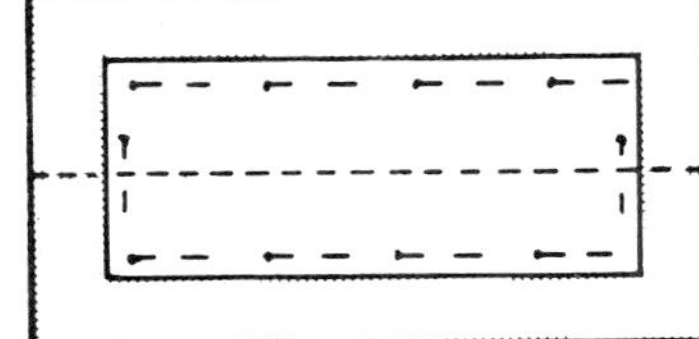

position. Snip at the corner as shown so that the fabric lies flat. With open herringbone, stitch the seam allowance to the interlining, cut a lining the same

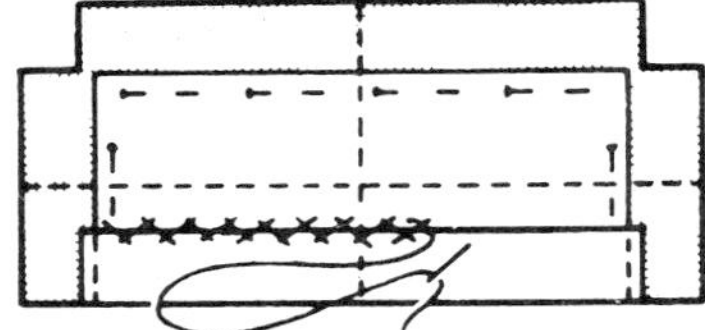

size as the decorated fabric, turn in slightly more than the seam allowance and slip stitch into position.

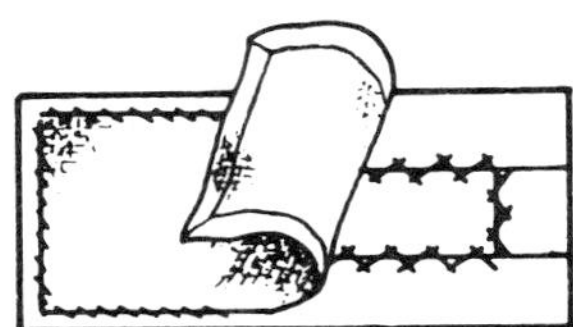

The glasses case. Interline and line the embroidered front and the back and overcast firmly on the right side over a matching cord. Be sure that the opening is large enough for the glasses to slip in easily.

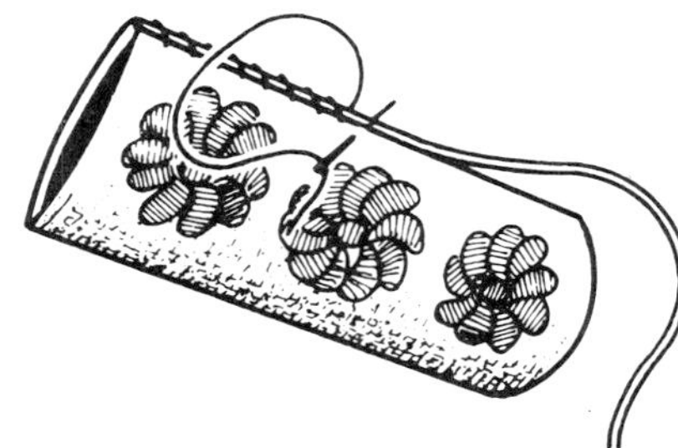

The belt. Make up as for the basic method and finish with pierced eyelet holes to carry the cord.

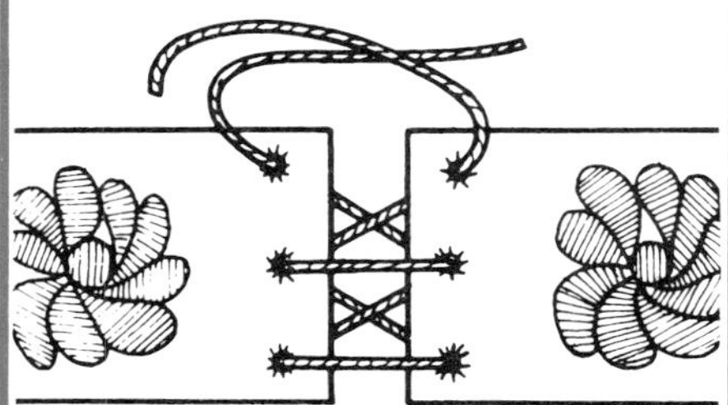

Marking circular cloths and mats

Measure and mark the center of the fabric. Cut a length of string, measuring from the center to the required extent of the circumference. Fasten a pencil at one end and a thumbtack at the other, fix the thumbtack at the center mark and draw the circle, keeping the string taut.

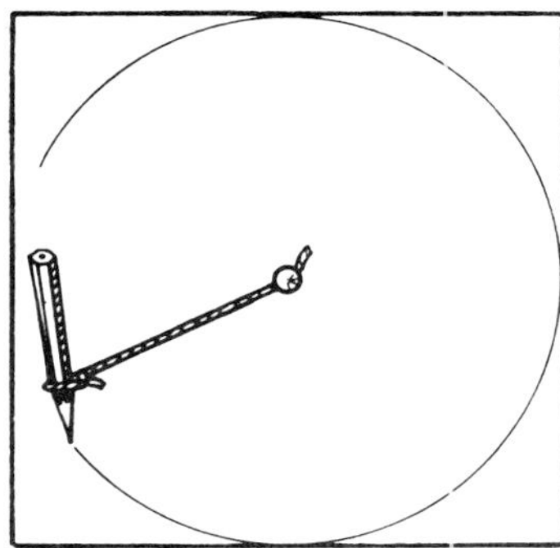

For a small circle, cut cardboard strip, at one end make a hole for pencil point and at the other fix a thumbtack. It may be used in the same way as the string and will accurately repeat a series of mats of the same size.

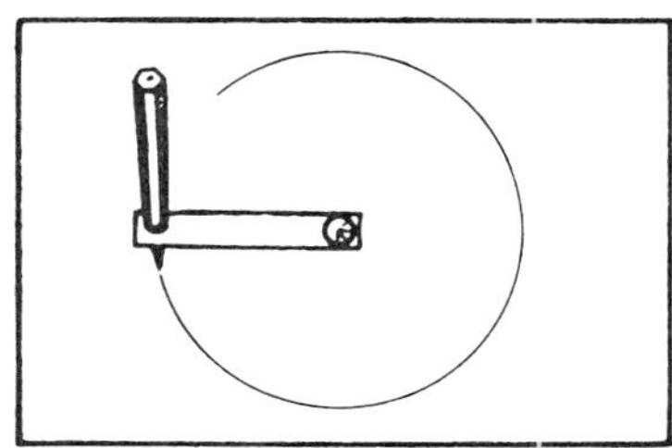

Joining the fabric for a large cloth. If the fabric has to be joined, stitch the seam and press open before marking the circle. Two side seams are less conspicuous and the circle may be cut from slightly less fabric if two side seams are stitched. Cut the length required, and divide the remaining piece down the center. Match centers of each piece and join the two half pieces, one each side of the whole. Press seams open, mark the circle as shown, and cut the circle and stitch the hem when the embroidery is complete.

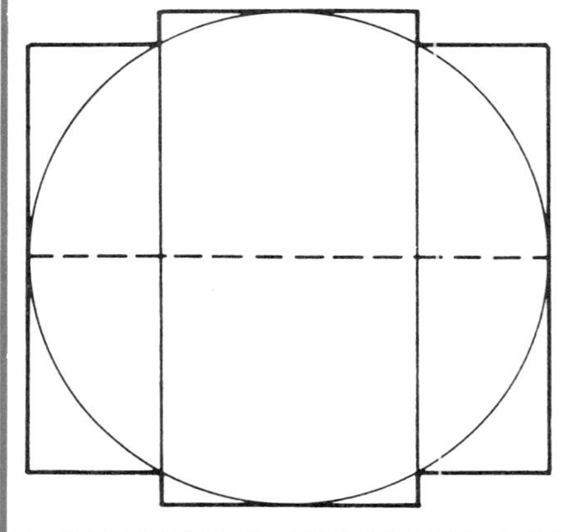

Finishing methods suitable for tablecloths, mats and bedspreads

An allowance of approximately $1\frac{1}{2}$ inches has been made on the fabric amounts given which allows for mounting in an embroidery frame and for blocking. Some of this allowance may need to be cut off when making up. Hems should relate in size to the weight of fabric – a smaller hem for lightweight than for heavy. On a fabric which frays easily make the first turning wider than normal.

Mitered corner and plain hem. Fold and press the hem, open out and fold the corner on the inner fold line, and cut off the corner, leaving a seam allowance. Refold the hem, slipstitch the miter and continue hemming.

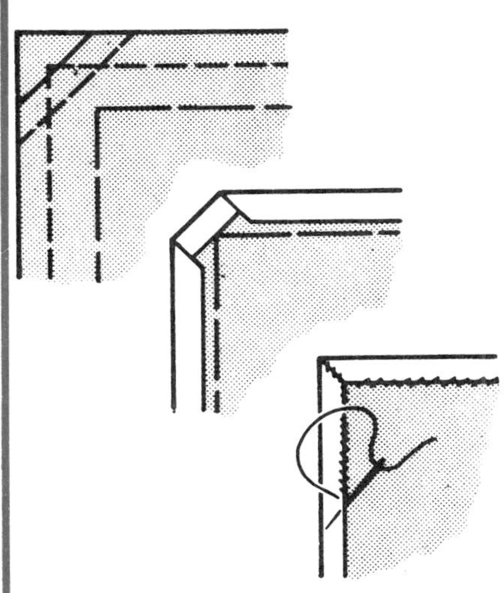

Fringe trimming. Pin the heading of the trimming to the hem line and machine or hand stitch firmly in place.

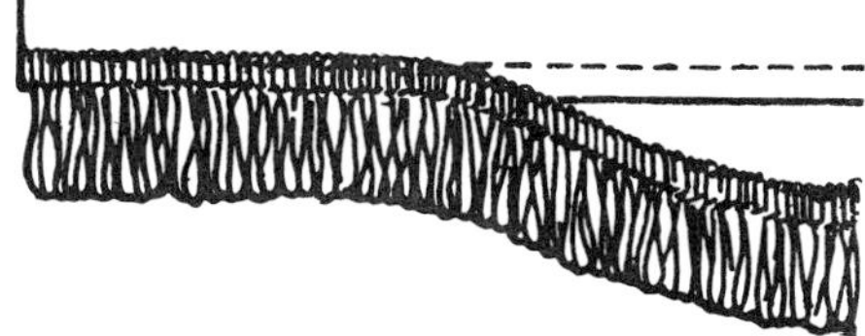

Finishing a curve. Before cutting the curve, run a gathering thread within the cutting line. Cut the curve and pull the

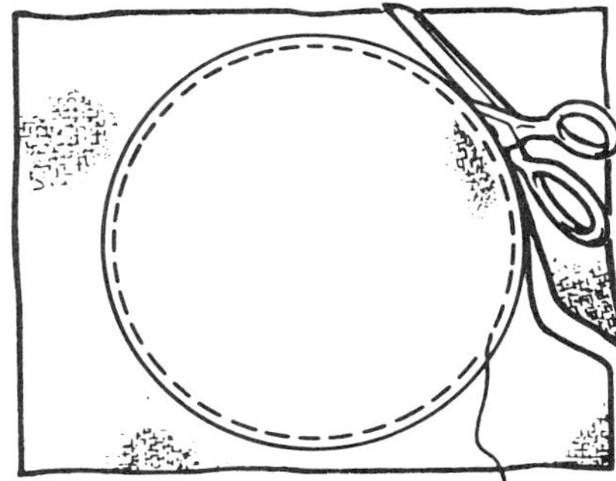

gathering thread slightly to take in the extra fabric on the turning. Fold, press and stitch the hem in the usual way.

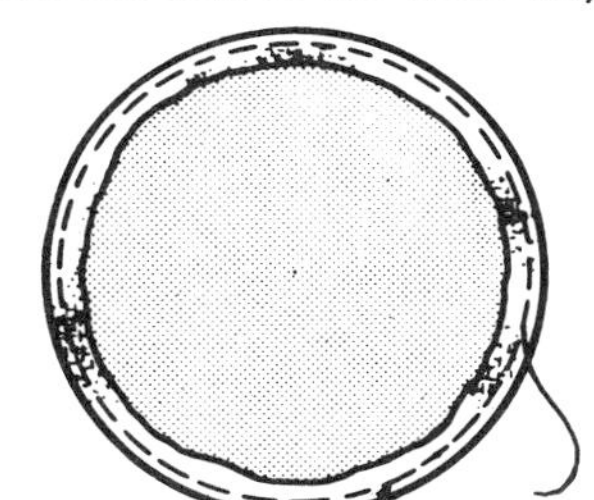

Binding a hem. For a concealed hem: Place the bias binding and the finished embroidery right sides together and machine stitch. Fold in the binding for

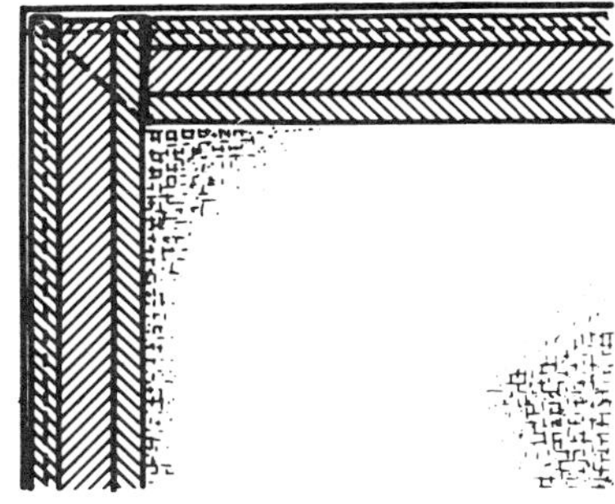

a neat corner. Turn to the wrong side of the fabric and slip stitch by hand. As a

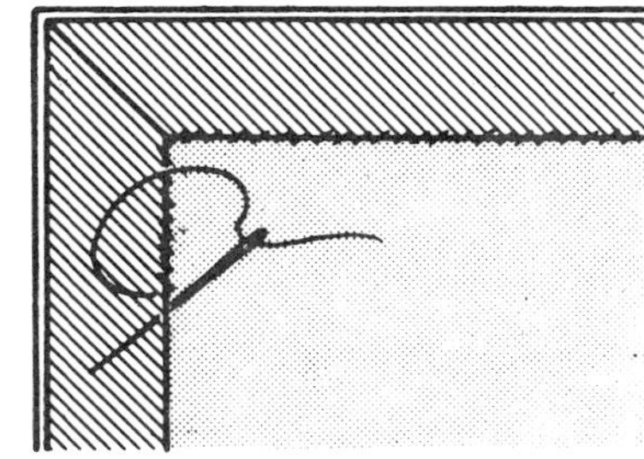

decorative finish (suitable for lightweight fabrics) fold the binding in half and baste over the edge of the fabric. Backstitch by hand or machine stitch.

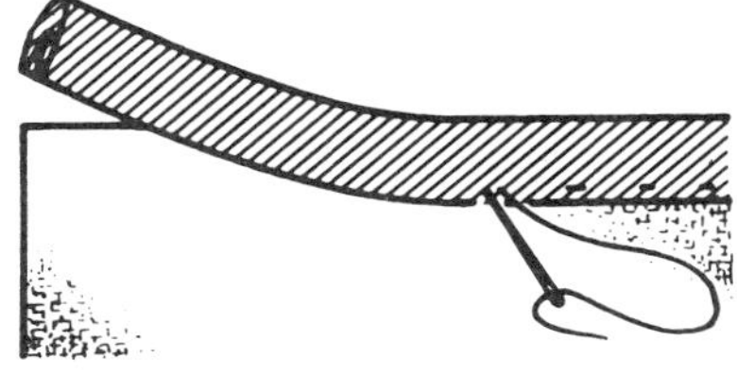

Needlepoint stool

To assess the amount of canvas, measure vertically and horizontally across the center of the stool, including the side drop. To each measurement allow at

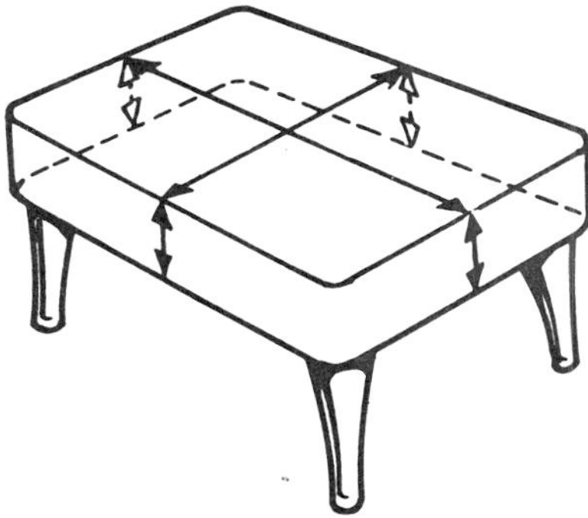

least 6 inches for blocking and making up. To mark the area of the canvas to be embroidered first measure the top of the stool. Outline this area with basting stitches on the canvas, and extend the horizontal and vertical lines at each side for the depth of the side drop. Work the embroidery within these lines.

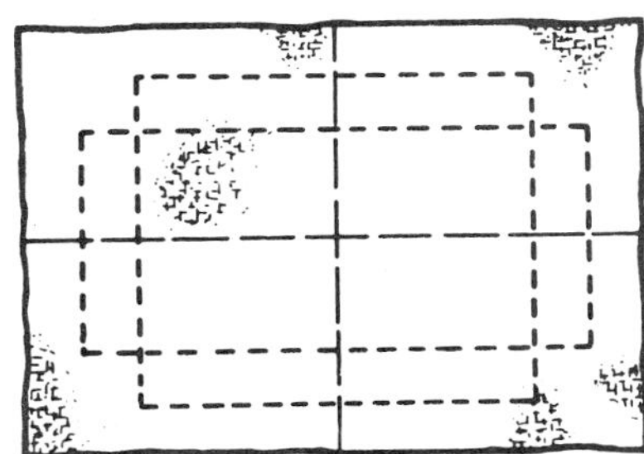

To cover the stool. Block the finished canvas, bring the right sides of the finished corners together as shown and backstitch close to the embroidery. Trim seam allowance at lower edge to $1\frac{1}{2}$ inches. Turn the corner triangles to one side. Herringbone the corner and seam

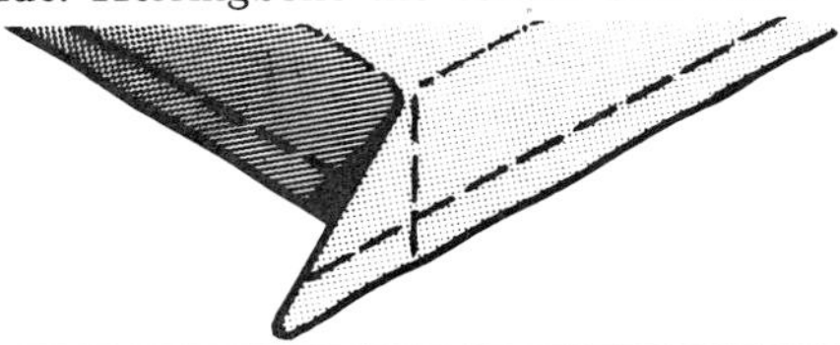

allowance in position at the back of the work. Turn to right side. Fit the cover to

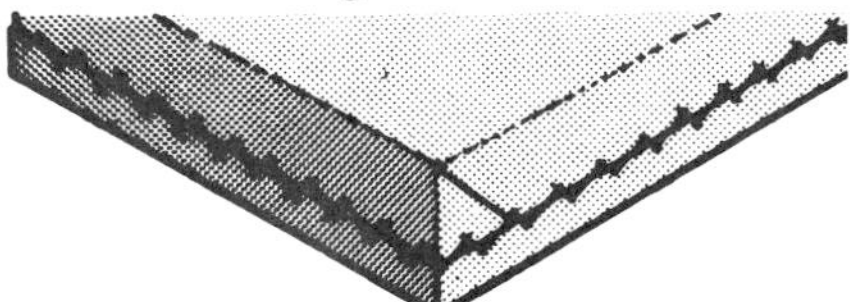

the stool. Working from the centers at each side, fix the canvas with brass headed tacks. Smooth the canvas into position as you work. Or, plain tacks may be used and a decorative braid fixed at intervals to conceal them.

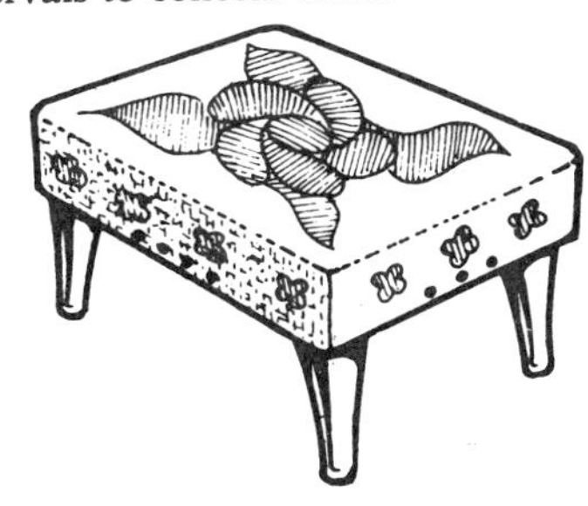

Making up pillows

Pillow forms and pillows are made to the same pattern to fit one within another. Make the pillow form ½ inch smaller in each direction so that the cover will fit smoothly and slip on and off for washing. Fill the pad with foam rubber chips or kapok.

Circular pillow. Stitch around seam-line right sides together, leaving an opening to insert filling. Cut out circle

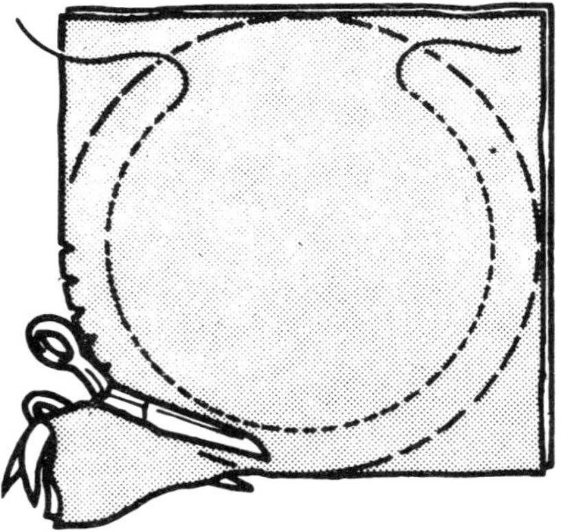

and clip at intervals for a smooth seam. Turn to right side, insert the form and overcast the remaining few inches with small stitches in matching thread.

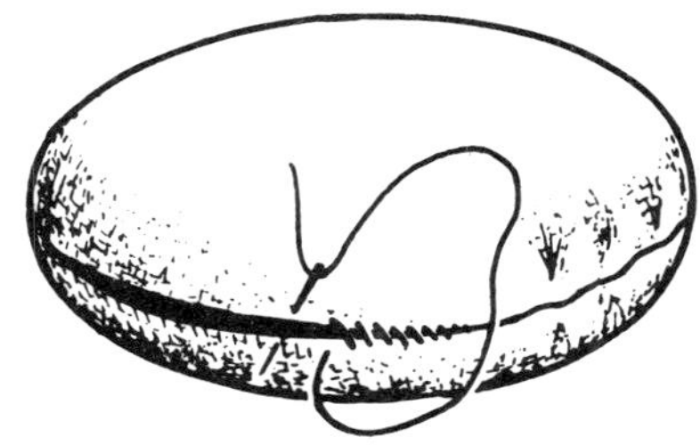

Square pillow. Make up in the same way. Clip corners and trim seam before turning to the right side.

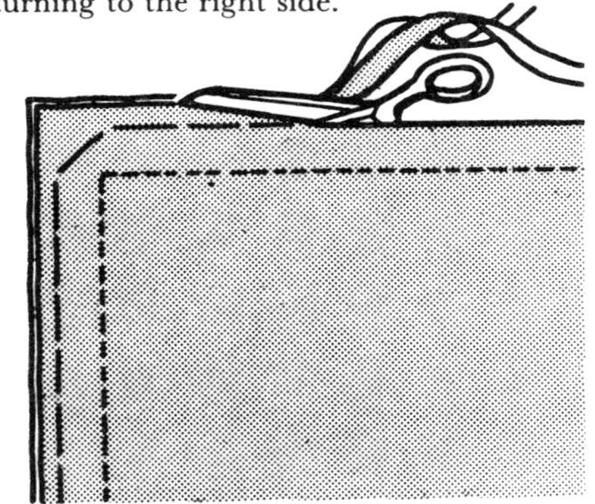

Pillow with gusset. Cut a strip of fabric of required width and length, plus seam allowance. Stitch the two ends, right sides together. With right sides together, stitch gusset to one side of the pillow. Repeat at the other side, leaving an opening to insert the form.

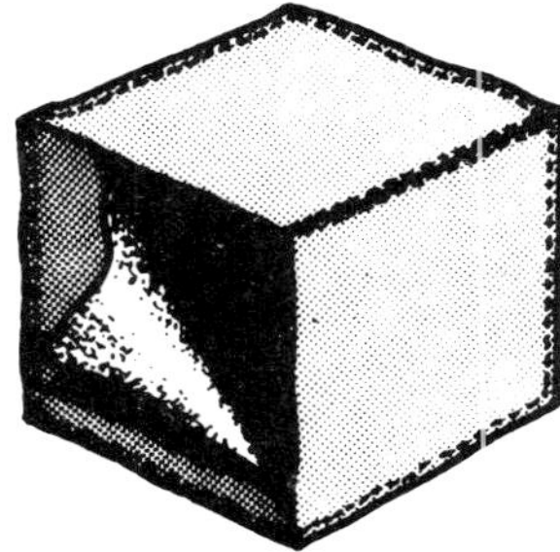

Trim seams and clip at corners. Turn to right side. Insert form or filling and overcast as for the plain pillow.

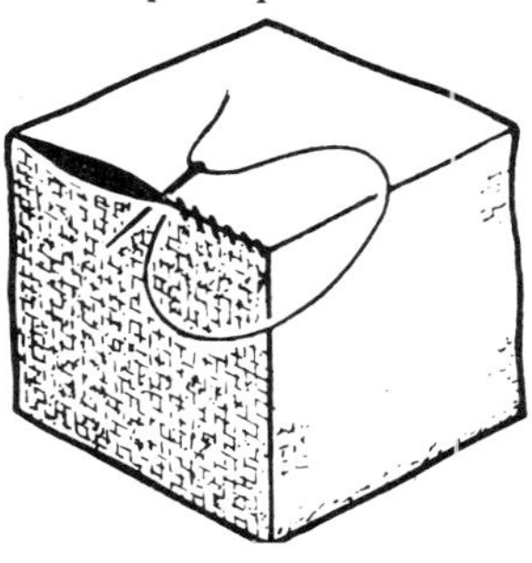

Handbag with inset cross-stitch panel

From the brown linen 24″ x 18″, cut a strip 5 inches wide for the handle. On

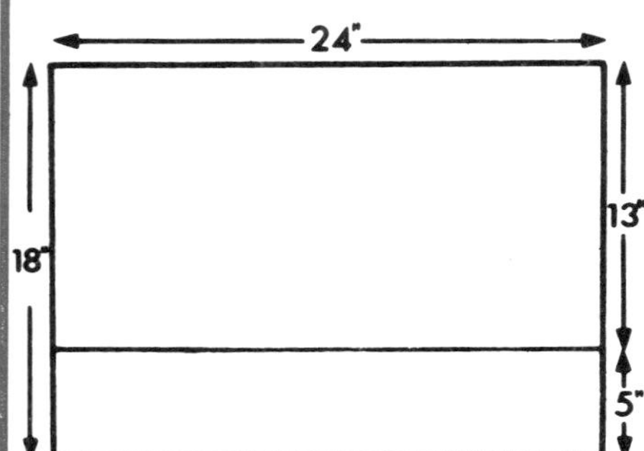

the remaining 13 inch width, mark the base of the bag and the area of the inset embroidery with basting lines, allowing half inch turning. Keeping exactly to the thread of the fabric, cut out the panel

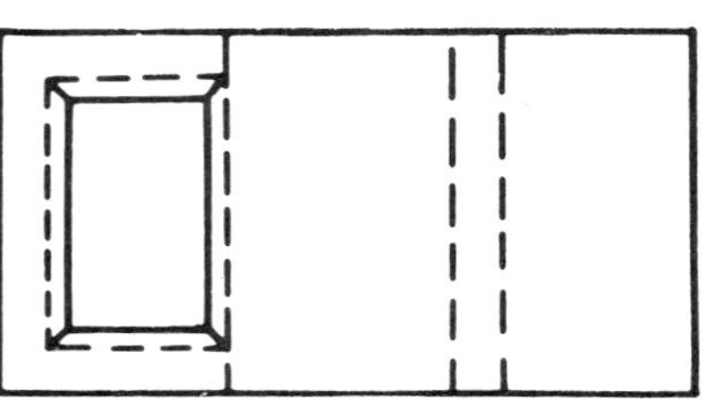

within the turning. Baste embroidered panel into position behind the cut away panel, clip the linen at the corners, turn in the hem and stab stitch securely.

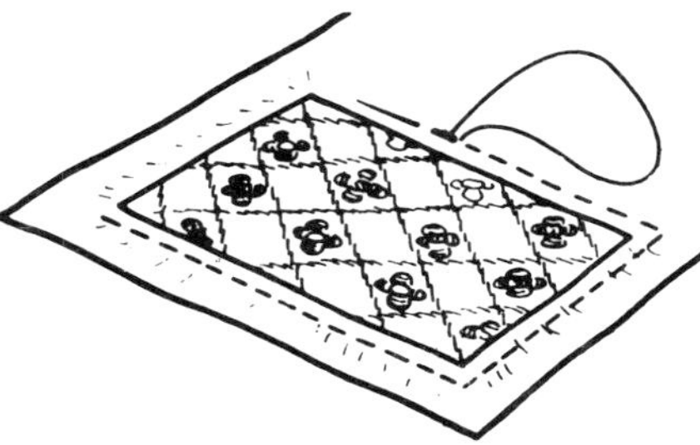

Interline and line as on page 122. For the handle, cut the 5 inch strip in half lengthwise. Seam the two narrow ends right sides together, and press seam open.

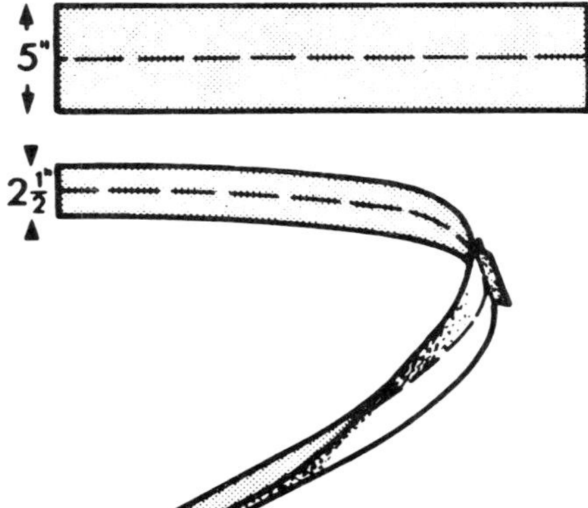

Stitch long seam, right sides together, turn and press. Fit one end to basted

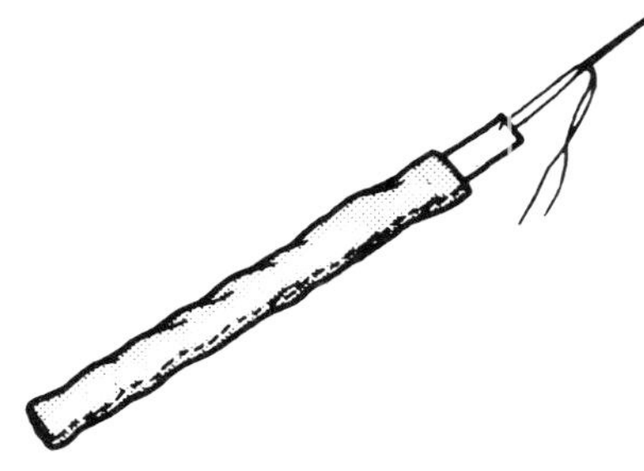

base line and pin at base and sides. Adjust the length of handle to the size required and insert at the opposite side. Stab stitch the handle and sides together.

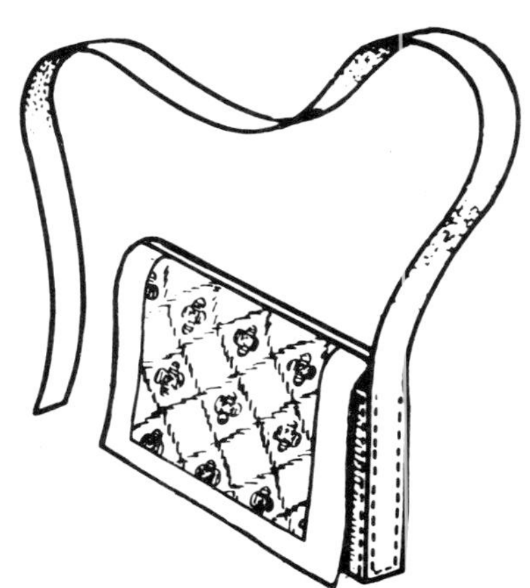

Making the kneelers

Fold the worked canvas along the unworked threads and embroider these with long-armed cross-stitch. Seam the

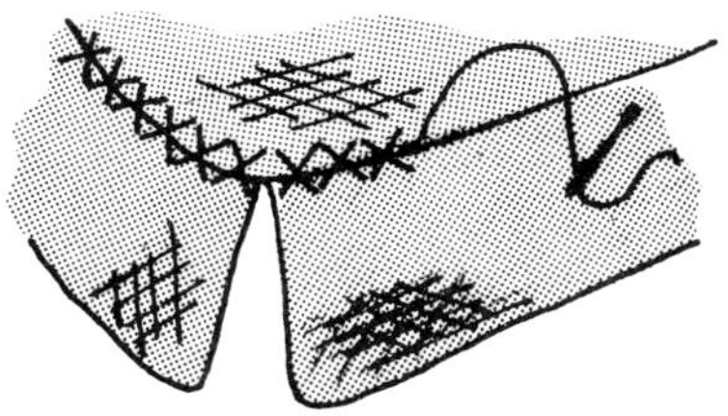

corners very firmly on the wrong side, either by hand or with two accurate rows of machine stitching, one on top

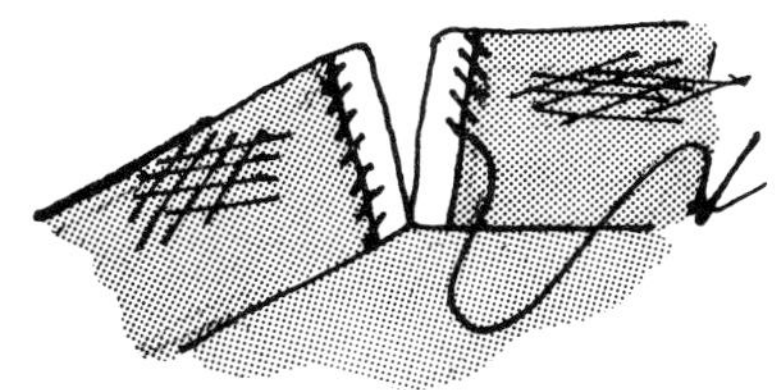

of the other for strength. Trim the seam and overcast raw edges. Turn the kneeler to the right side and work long-armed cross-stitch over the corner seams.

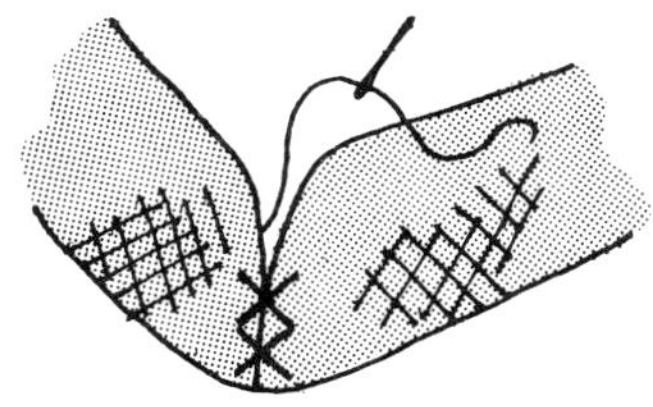

The padding can be either layers of carpet felt, or a piece of foam rubber or plastic foam, but the pad must be ½ inch larger than the kneeler's finished size in all measurements. Place the padding inside the kneeler and push it firmly into the corners. Lace the canvas over the padding on the back, using strong, fine string, beginning with the two long sides and finishing with the two short sides. Trim and make the corners neat

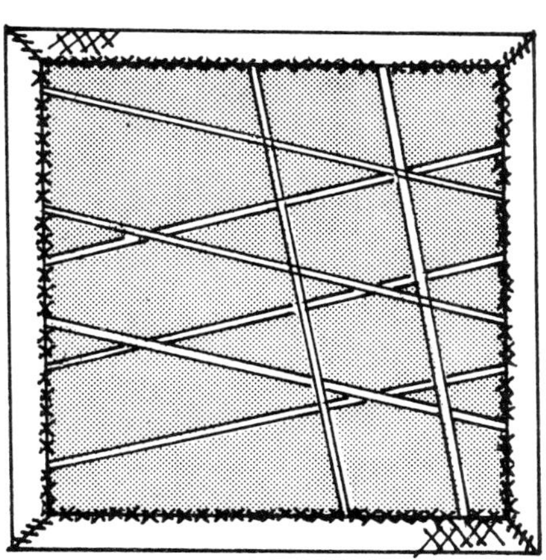

by overcasting. Cover the base of the kneeler with upholsterer's black lining fabric or other sturdy lining.
If the kneeler is to be hung, sew a large

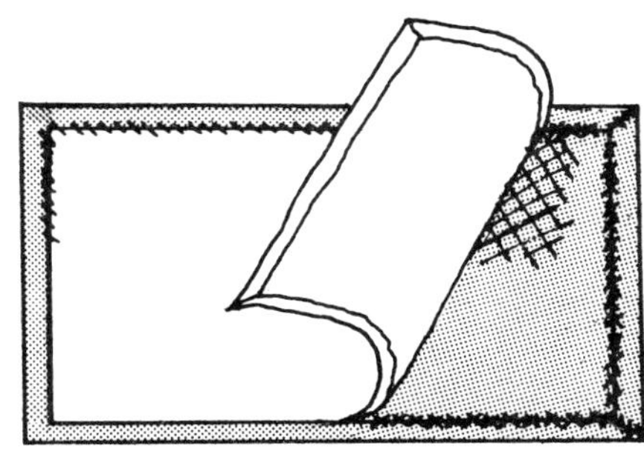

curtain ring to the edge of the kneeler, stitching through base lining and canvas.

Making the framed picture and the pillow

Preparing the picture for framing
Cut a hole 9 inches square in the center of the 15½ inch square sage green fabric. Cut a hole 10 inches square in the center of one of the pieces of mat board. Snip into the corners of the fabric mount as before and mount the sage green fabric onto the mat board, mitering the corners and securing the fabric on the back of the mount with small spots of glue. Mount the embroidered linen on the second piece of mat board. Frame in a deep frame.

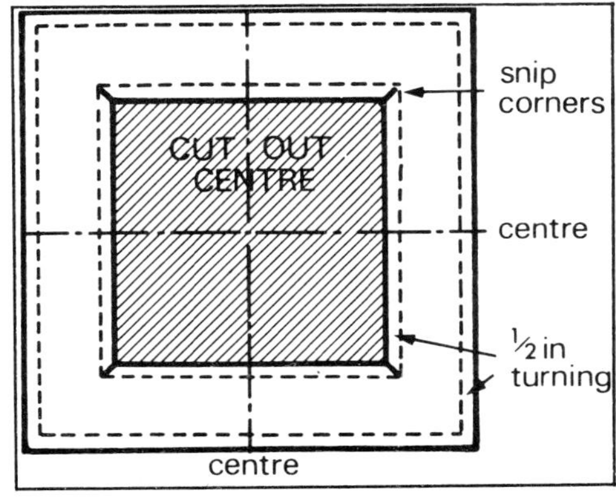

Making the pillow
Press the finished embroidery. From the 15 inch square sage green fabric cut a 9 inch square from the center. Snip ½ inch into the corners of the remaining fabric frame. Turn in the edge and press. Matching centers, baste the square mount in position over the embroidery and using matching thread, stab stitch the two together. Work a small stitch on the surface and a larger underneath. Couch six strands of oak brown thread where the edge of the mount touches the embroidery. Make the pillow in the usual way.

stitch library

The stitches shown are easily worked. Allow the threads to lie easily on the surface of the fabric. It should not be pulled out of shape by the stitch. To prevent threads from knotting: With a woolen thread stitch in the direction of the natural lie of the wool. Run a hand along the thread. In one direction the hairs lie flatter than in the other. For 6-strand floss: cut the length of thread, not more than 18 inches for a trouble-free needleful. Divide at the center for the number of strands required. They will separate easily without knotting.

Stem stitch

Use for straight and curved lines. Notice the position of the thread for left- and right-hand curves. Begin on the traced line and work inward when used to fill a shape.

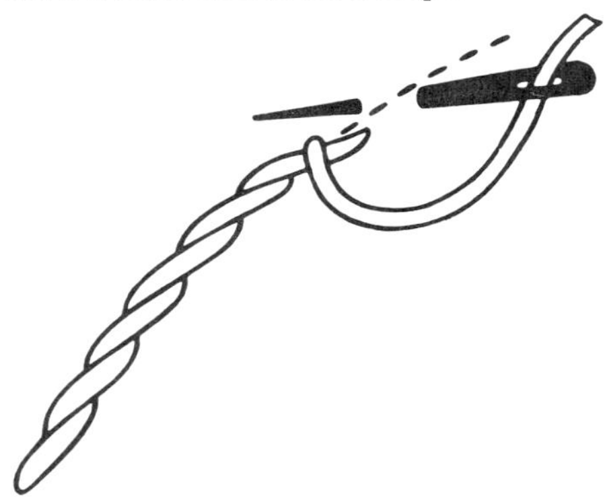

French knot

To make a well-shaped knot, as the needle returns into the fabric, keep the thread taut.

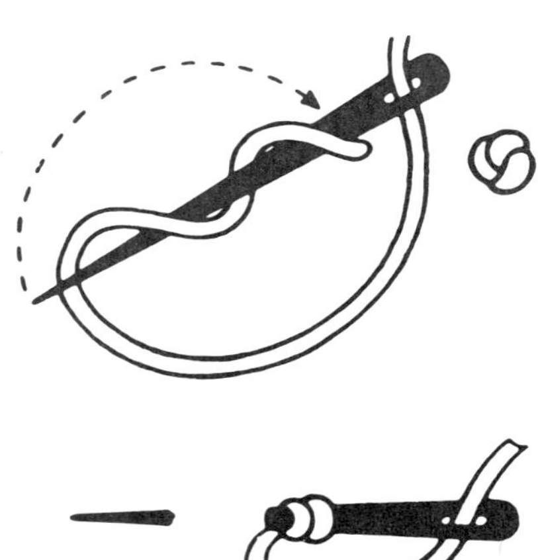

Cross-stitch

For an even appearance, work one row below another. The stitches should cross in the same direction throughout the work.

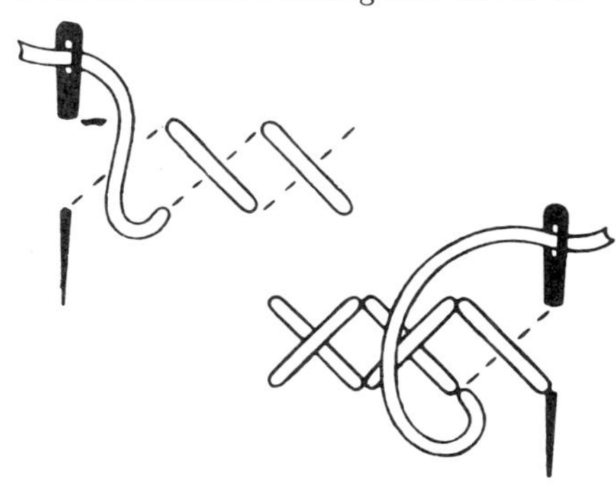

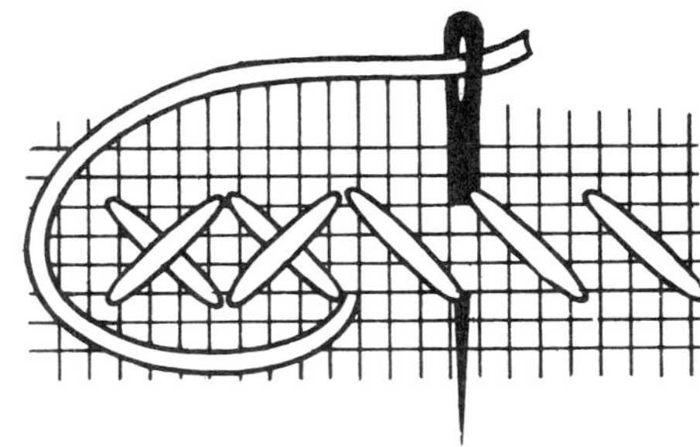

Herringbone stitch (closed)

The movements of the needle are the same as for open herringbone stitch, but the needle comes out close to the previous stitch.

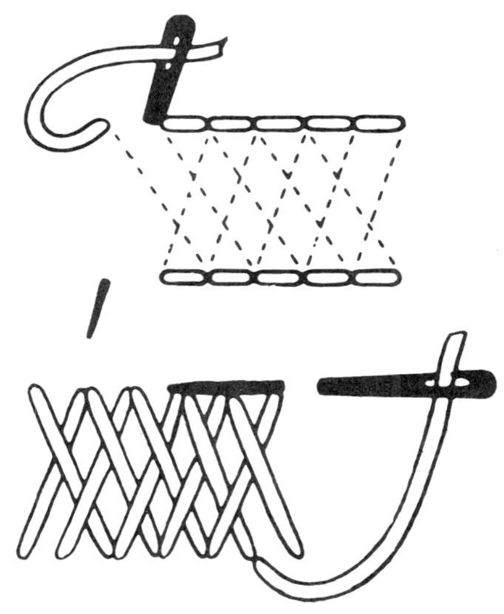

Herringbone stitch (open)

Work vertically upward, or from left to right.

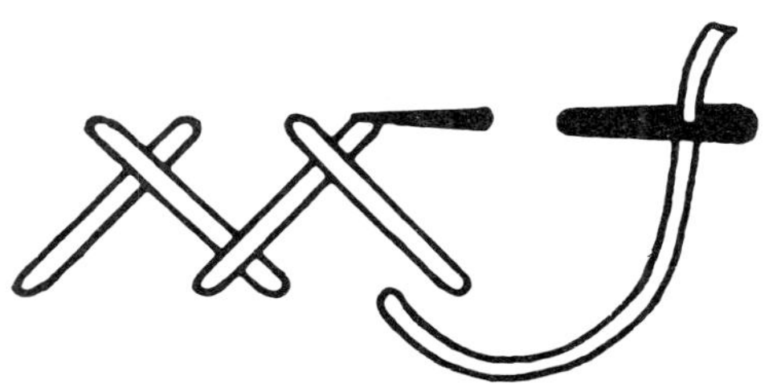

Feather stitch (half)

The needle goes in to one side of the previous stitch. The position of the needle and thread is the same as in chain stitch.

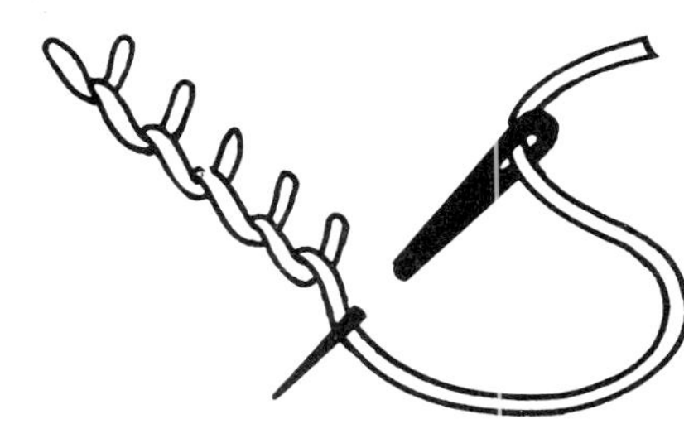

Long and short stitch

Work it as in the diagram for a broken surface. For a smooth surface, work the first row as shown. On the second row, bring the needle UP through the previous stitch. Best worked in a frame.

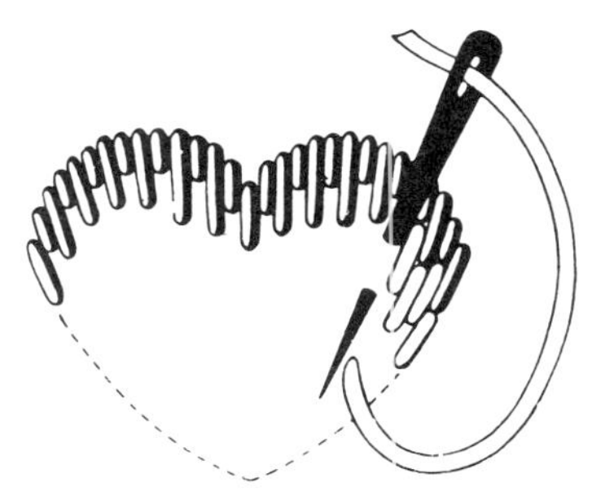

Rumanian stitch

Take a long stitch across the shape to be worked and tie it down with a slanting stitch.

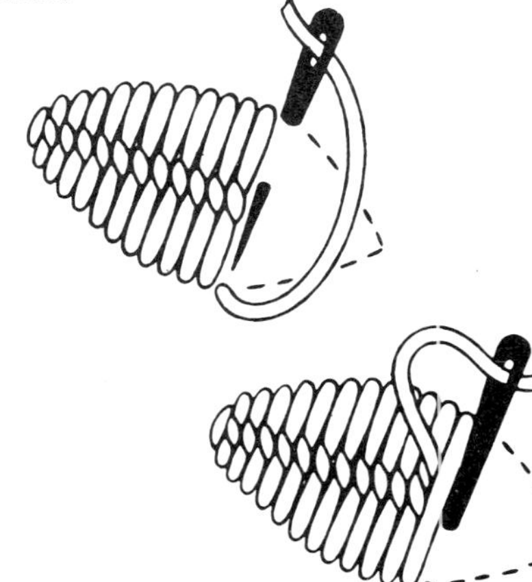

Running stitch

Use the stitch as an outline, or in rows as filling stitch.

Satin stitch

Most easily worked in a frame. The movements of the needle are simple. Hold the thread in position before inserting the needle. The stitches will lie smoothly side by side. For a raised effect, first pad with running stitches.

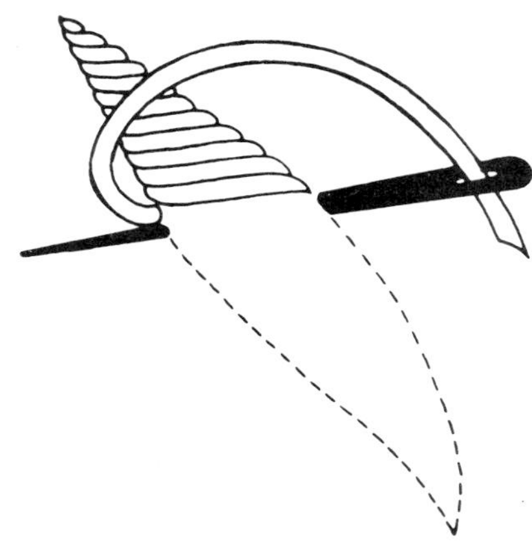

Surface satin stitch

Economical in thread. In relation to satin stitch, it has a slightly broken surface.

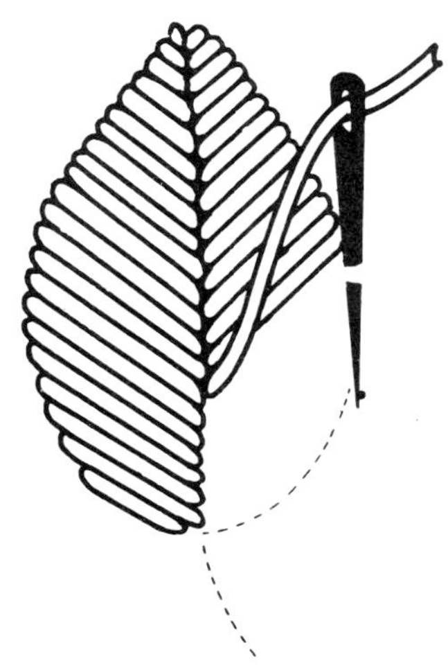

Slip stitch

Holds the hem in position with very little stitching showing on the right side.

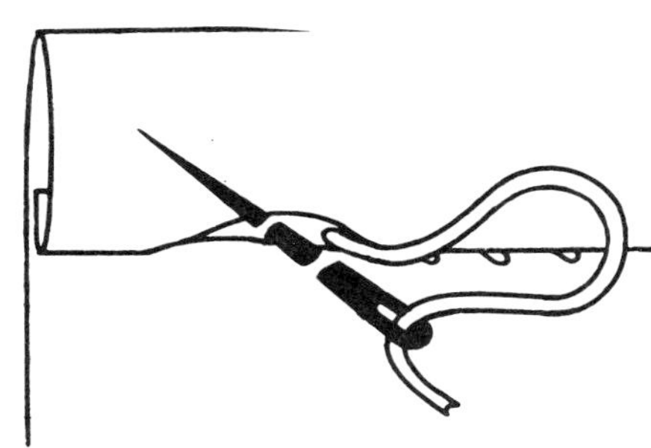

Blanket stitch

The thread loops underneath the needle which lies vertically in the fabric.

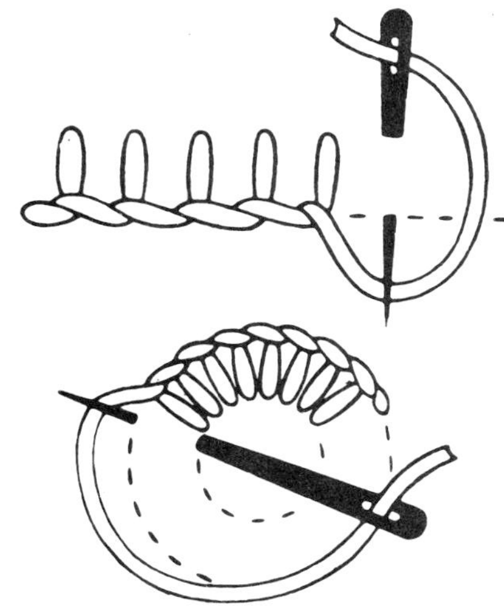

Chain stitch

The needle returns to the place where it came out. The thread loops under it. Chain stitch may be worked in straight or curved lines. Use it in circles or rows to fill a shape. When used as a filling, begin at the outer edge and work inward.

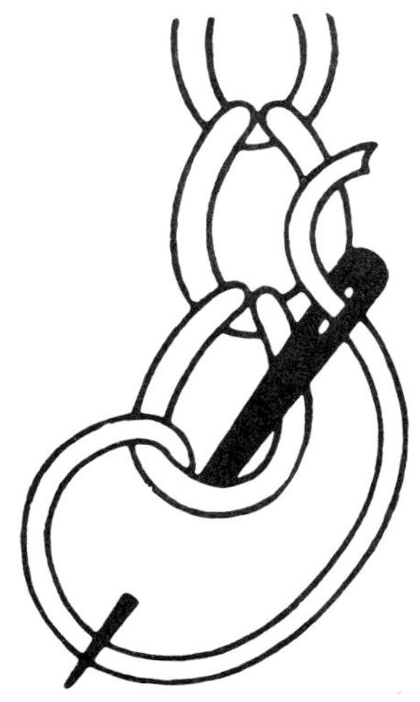

Detached chain

Each stitch is held down separately with the working thread. Finish a row of chain stitch in this manner. The method for making a point in a line of chain stitch is also shown.

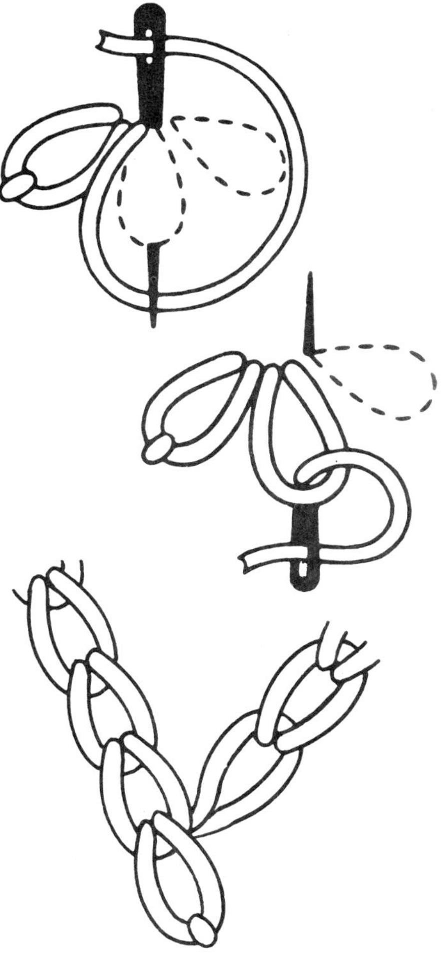

Couching

More easily worked with the fabric in a frame. With a large needle, take a thick thread to the back of the fabric. On the surface, tie it down with small stitches in a color-matched, thin thread. If the embroidery is to be laundered, stitch at frequent intervals to prevent the line pulling out of shape. Work it as a single line or in rows.

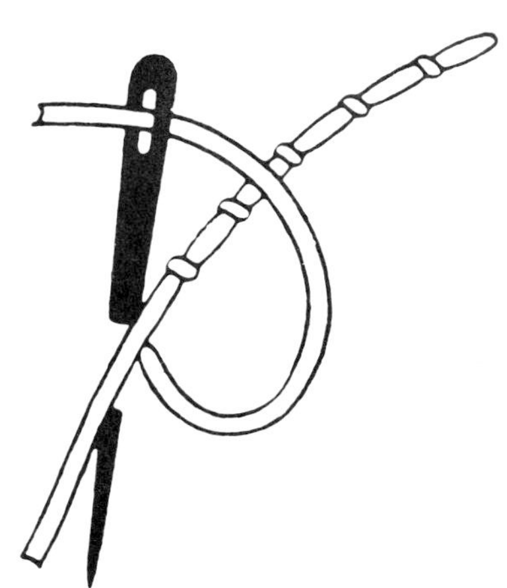

Back Stitch

Bring the thread through on the stitch line, then take a small backward stitch through the fabric. Bring the needle through again a little in front of the first stitch, take another stitch, inserting the needle at the point where it first came through.

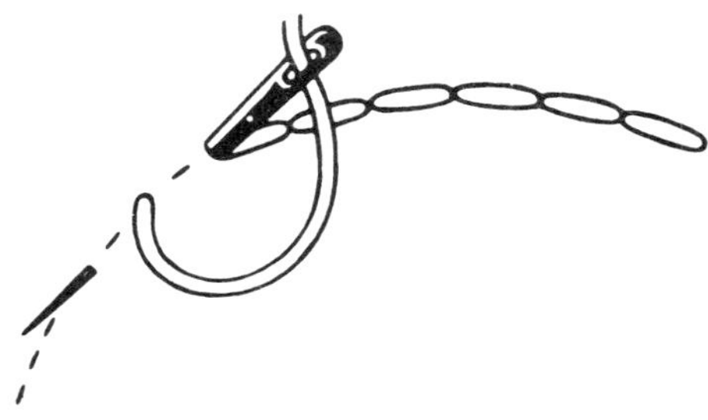

Whipped Back Stitch

This stitch is worked from right to left and is generally used in Spanish Blackwork Embroidery for outlining a design.
Work Back Stitch (see above) first, then with another needle in the thread, whip over each Back Stitch without entering the fabric.

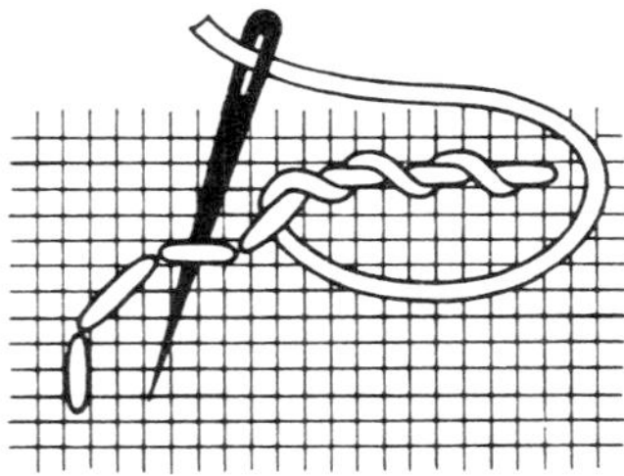

Brick Stitch

This stitch is worked in rows alternately from left to right. The first row consists of long and short stitches into which are fitted rows of even Satin Stitches, thus giving a "brick" formation. The whole filling must be worked very regularly, making each Satin Stitch of even length and all exactly parallel.

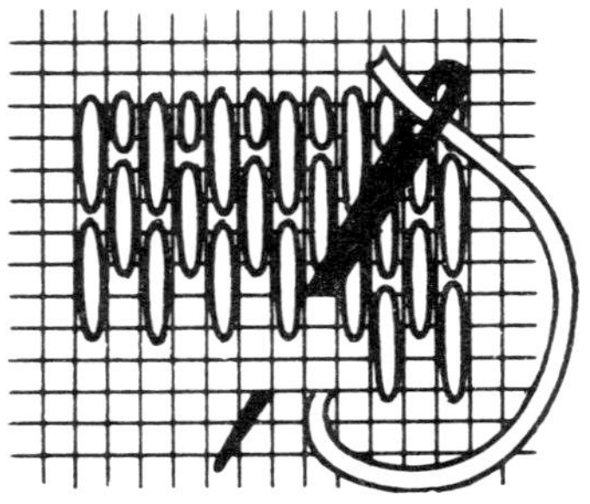

Rice Stitch

This stitch is usually worked in a thick embroidery thread for the large Cross Stitch (see page 126) and a fine thread for the small Straight Stitch. Fig. 1—first cover the area required with Cross Stitch worked over four threads each way of the canvas. Fig. 2—over the corners of each Cross Stitch work small diagonal stitches at right angles over two threads each way of the canvas, so that these small stitches also form a cross. The small stitches are shown black in order to show the construction.

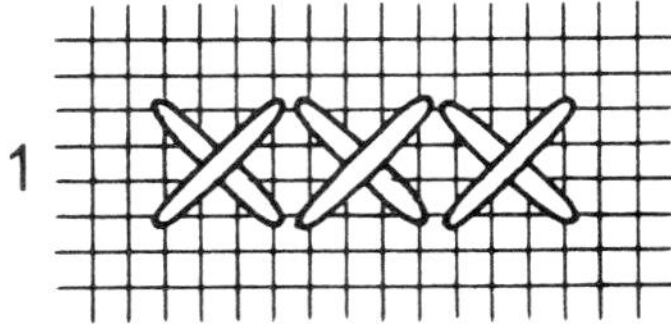

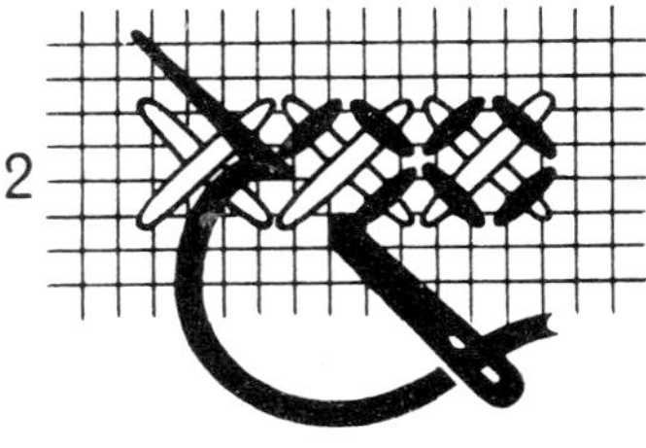

Holbein Stitch

Holbein Stitch is sometimes called Double Running Stitch. Working from right to left, work a row of Running Stitch (see page 127) over and under three threads of fabric, following the shape of the design. On the return journey, work in the same way from left to right, filling in the spaces left in the first row. This stitch is used in Assisi Embroidery to outline the Cross Stitch, but may also be used in other types of designs on evenweave fabric.

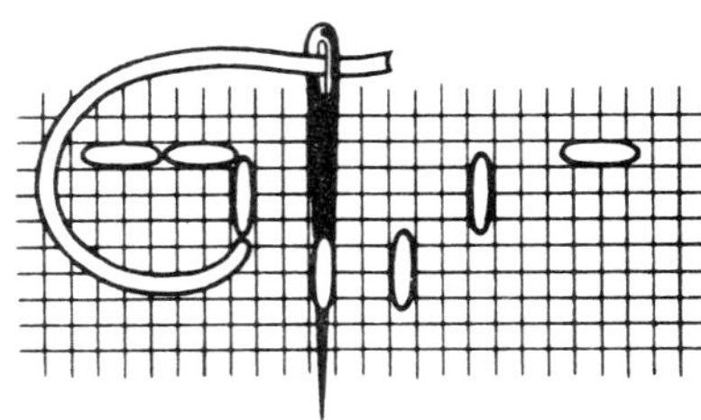

Canvas Stitches

Petit Point is the stitch used on a fine single thread canvas, while Gros Point is suitable for the slightly heavier double thread canvas, and both come under the general name of Tent Stitch.
A trammed stitch may be used with Gros Point to ensure that the threads of the canvas are completely covered. This will also give a neater appearance to the work.

Trammed Gros Point Stitch

Fig. 1—work a Trammed Stitch from left to right, then pull the needle through and insert again up and over the crossed threads. Fig. 2—pull the needle through on the lower line two double threads (vertical) to the left in readiness for the next stitch.
Method of working Gros Point Stitch using both hands. With right hand on top of canvas, insert the needle downwards through the canvas and pull the needle through with the left hand. With left hand, push the needle upwards through the canvas and pull out with the right hand.

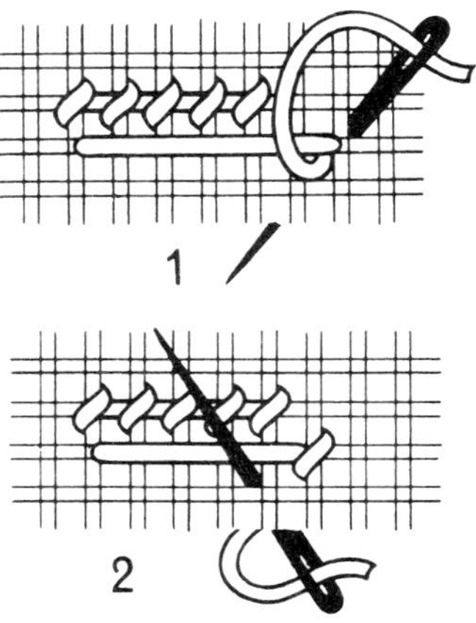

Petit Point Stitch

Fig. 1—bring the thread out on the left-hand side of the fabric on the top part of the first stitch; pass the needle down diagonally over the crossed threads, then under two threads, continue in this way to complete the row. Fig. 2—the second row is worked from right to left, the needle passing the crossed threads up and over, then under two threads. Work backwards and forwards in this way until the design is complete. All stitches should slope in the same direction. The stitches on the reverse side are longer and slope more than on the correct side.

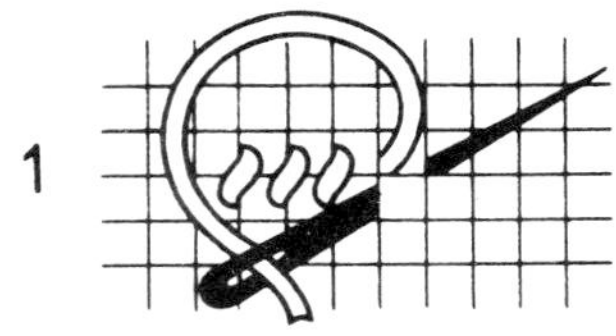

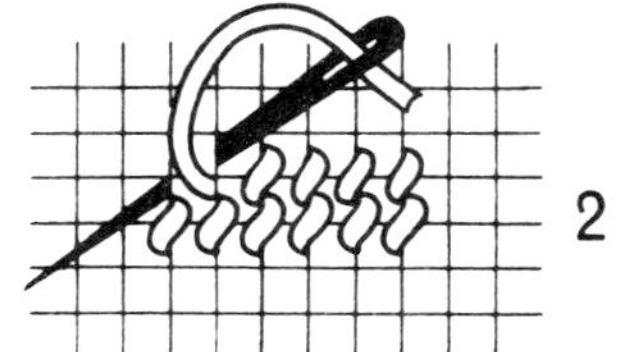